CRY OF THE PHOENIX

Colleen O'Connor

Cat's Eye Enterprises Ltd.
Vancouver, Canada

First Published in Canada in 2007 by
Cat's Eye Enterprises Ltd.

Copyright 2007, Cat's Eye Enterprises Ltd.
First Canadian Edition
Cover Work by Philippe Brunel
Cover Design by Philip Rivest

The moral right of the author has been asserted.

Library and Archives Canada Cataloguing in Publications

O'Connor, Colleen, 1947-
Cry of the phoenix / Colleen O'Connor

ISBN 978-0-9783988-0-4

1. O'Connor, Colleen, 1947- 2. O'Connor, Colleen, 1947- --Family.
3. Women justices of the peace--British Columbia--Biography. I. Title.
BF637.S4O218 2007   347.711'016   C2007-905029-8

Cat's Eye Enterprises Ltd. is committed to protecting the environment
and the responsible use of natural resources. We are acting on this
commitment by working with suppliers and printers to phase out paper
produced from ancient forests. This book is printed on 100% ancient
forest-free paper (100% post-consumer recycled), processed chlorine
and acid-free. It is printed with vegetable-based inks.
Printed and bound in Canada by Friesens

This book is dedicated to the following
who have been a support to me:

Liam Rivest, who taught me to open
my heart and let love enter.

Philip Rivest, who has come to mean so
much to me over the past years.

John L. Daly, who kept me at my book. As
you said: the story has to be told.

The beautiful, mystical Phoenix bird is bright orange and red in colour. The Phoenix is the bird of the astrological sign of Scorpio, the sign under which I was born. It is the bird of transformation. In Egyptian mythology it is a bird of gorgeous plumage, sacred to the sun, and is known as the Sun Bird.

The Phoenix is reborn from the ashes of the funeral pyre which it makes for itself when each life span of approximately 500 years is over. At the top of a palm tree the bird's nest catches fire, ignited by a spark struck by the hooves of celestial steeds drawing the chariot of Ra, the Egyptian Sun God.

Amid the flames the beautiful bird extends its golden neck and purple wings; instead of flying off, it dances. Eventually, the Phoenix is consumed by fire and is reduced to ashes. But this is not the end: a new Phoenix chick arises out of the ashes and spreads its beautiful wings to fly again as the magnificent mystical Phoenix.

The patterns of our lives follow the life and death of the mystical Phoenix. I know that the Phoenix has been here with me; every time I am in trouble or in strife the Phoenix sings to me with its beautiful, melodic, throaty song and sends me its hot tears to help me through my pain. Although I did not know it nor understand, the Phoenix has been with me at all times.

Chapter One

Two o'clock in the morning is the darkest hour for me. That is the time when the loneliness comes on. I wake and there is no one in the house but myself. Dawn is hours away, and I know any attempt at sleep is futile. Two o'clock in the morning is the darkest hour for me because that is when the ghosts crowd in, each one with his or her own story, and I'm given the lonely duty to make peace among them. You have to be strong—or foolhardy—to take this on: to rake through the past, digging among the ashes for something of significance to appease the voices, to quiet them. The search is not for the faint-hearted.

If there is one thing I tell myself not to do—at any time of the day or night—it's to look back. For me, the present has far more purpose. And I've learned there isn't much anyone can do about the past. What's gone is done, as they say. This writing, then, is an exception, a recognition of that time of night when one is alone and the voices from the past are the loudest, and the most plaintive.

My name is Colleen O'Connor. I have been a Justice of the Peace for the Province of British Columbia for eighteen years.

Once, at a party, a woman extended her hand to me, and exclaimed, Oh, so you *marry* people . . .

No, I replied, as her dewy hand released mine. I do something a little different. I put them in jail.

She seemed a little chagrined.

I suggested that maybe there wasn't a big difference between the two.

I can say that in the years I've been a Justice I've had my eyes opened. Literally. When the police needed a search warrant in the middle of the night, it was me they called. And, even as I shook off sleep, I needed to make sure the police officer who was calling had good reason for doing so. You don't hand out a search warrant just because someone asks for it.

Nine times out of ten, the next day in court the accused would stand before me. Then, it was up to me again to make a decision: should the accused go home or stay the weekend at the taxpayers' expense?

As it is given, my story is not a matter of fiction. All the events of which I write did occur. I have written about them as best as I remember, with the understanding that they are necessarily limited to one perspective—my own. I have changed the names of the people who appear here so as to protect their right to privacy. In some cases, I have changed certain details so that the larger story may be told.

The story I present is one which I could never have predicted, given its twists and turns, and the design of which remains a mystery to me still. I write for those whose story, in some way, is similar to mine. Do not lose heart, dear friend, I say. Do not lose heart.

I feel that, if anything, my story, is a lesson in how one can overcome life's obstacles, those limitations imposed by others—and most of all—those imposed by oneself. If one reader gains something useful from the story I am about to tell, I will be more than satisfied.

Today, to travel from Vancouver up the fjord of Howe Sound is less than a morning's drive. The Sea-to-Sky Highway is fast and busy, connecting West Vancouver at the mouth of the Sound to Squamish at its farthest reach. Whistler, with its skiing opportunities and world-class resort, lies still further beyond.

Years ago, however, there was no highway—not even a road. Instead, like my parents, one boarded the Union Steamship in Vancouver. The ship carried you up the Sound as far as the port of Squamish. The trip was seven hours, a total of seventy miles, Vancouver to Squamish, and return.

Anyone who has traveled the Sound knows its beauty. There is the jewel of Bowen Island at the mouth of the Sound, then Gambier, a darker and still larger gem, and Anvil, darker still. Along the way you cannot help but notice Mount Sheer. It rises powerfully from the water's edge. Its imposing profile, thousands of feet in height, dominates the shore. At the farthest reach of the Sound you see brilliant blue, snow-crested mountains. Eagles, their wings outstretched, pass high above.

If I could choose to go back in time, it would be to a day in late November many years ago. I suppose it was a day cold and crisp, as November days on the coast often are, with the water of the fjord green and cold as glacier water.

I am three weeks old, just out of hospital, an infant in my father's arms. I imagine myself, bundled in a warm blanket against the cold. The Union Steamship pulls in to Britannia Beach to unload its passengers.

Britannia Beach is the site of a copper and zinc mine that shipped all over the world. Even to this day, you can see the huge compressor that processed the ore. It is a huge building, eight tiers in height, fallen into disuse and disrepair, a site of historic interest, and often visited by tourists.

On the day of my arrival, we depart the ship. My parents walk down the dock to the end of a railway track. There, a flat bed rail car waits. The skip, which the flat bed is called, is used to bring the ore taken from the mine to the compressor and to carry groceries and supplies to the town site. On each side of the skip are horizontal metal cables. The skip has no seats. Instead of sitting, my parents stand along with the other passengers, gripping the cable nearest them and leaning against each other for support, as the skip jerks forward and starts its ascent. I am told that, given the steepness of the incline, the trip up the mountain—and down—could be quite frightening. I have no memory of it, but have a lifelong fear of heights and an enduring love of open spaces.

The town site of Mount Sheer itself was fairly drab. This was a company town. The houses were much the same color, yellow and brown, the same size and of the same design. A reservoir which was glacier-fed provided the water for the town and for the mine itself. The town had not much more than a general store and a community hall.

I was born with carrot red hair full of curls, and a million freckles. I was named after my dad's girlfriend. So, it comes as no surprise: even before I was born, there was already trouble in the works.

My dad was a very popular person. For one thing, every Saturday night at the community hall he played drums in the dance band. All the couples in town came out. My dad was also the projectionist at the movie theatre which once a week featured the latest movie. When my dad was not working in the mine, he preferred to dress up, walking about the town in a white shirt, tie, and dress slacks.

They must have been a couple to look at, my mom and my dad. My mom was a striking woman with dark, wavy hair, blue eyes, and high cheekbones. My mother prided herself on being a socialite of the town, going from one social event to the other, to teas and fundraisers and the like. She liked to go out in high heels, and she liked to be seen.

One of my early memories is of my mom brushing her hair at the oval mirror of her vanity. Vanity—that word captures so much of my mother's nature. In her own estimation, she was not beautiful—or, at least, not beautiful enough. She considered her cheekbones her best feature. She did what she could to add to her good looks. She was careful to watch her figure. To accentuate her slim waistline, she chose light, filmy dresses to wear. I would have to say that her diligence, and perseverance, paid off. I was always struck by the final presentation: to my eyes, my mother looked starved. And beautiful.

The problem between my mother and me perhaps came down partly to this—I was a dismal failure in the looks department. I was a stocky child with red curls and a large, freckled face. All the dressing up in the world was not going to make me beautiful. God knows my mother tried, with crinolines, and dresses, and holiday outfits, but none of them did anything but herald loudly how plain I was. I was a child my mother had not wanted. That point was drummed home to me on countless occasions. How could this have happened to my mother? To have a little girl she could not dress up, and fuss over, and be proud to be seen with?

I wonder now if the only reason my mother married my father was that she had gotten pregnant. If this was the case, it would have explained a lot. Every day of her married life my mother talked about how trapped she felt by her marriage. She had married, as she called it, "below her station". She regretted it terribly. And, as for me? Well, towards me, my mom always expressed a deliberate and outspoken dislike.

My mother went out about the town of Mount Sheer. I don't remember ever going with her. People about town would often see her out with my father. But then, my father was considered a good looking man in his day, and he was well liked.

My dad happened one day to bring home a live salmon. He put it in the bathtub, the idea being to keep it there until the time came for dinner. I was mesmerized by the creature. I leaned over the bathtub and petted it. The salmon flicked its fins, and moved away from me. I reached to touch it again, slipped and, before I knew it, was in the bathtub, too. The water was cold and, luckily, not very deep.

My father heard my cries and came to my rescue.

Swimming with the fishies, are you? he laughed, hoisting me up.

My clothes were wet and dripping. He took a towel and dried away my tears.

That'll teach you for being so curious.

To this day I cannot touch a fish. I don't like the feel of them. As for eating them, all it takes is two mouthfuls, and I feel ill.

My mom got restless and bored with living in the small town of Mount Sheer and decided we should move. It was the last thing my dad wanted to do. But my mom insisted. She had her reasons for leaving.

It was one of their regular Saturday night fights. It was always pretty much the same script. My parents' roles never seemed to vary. My mom would always get it going.

I'm fed up, Charlie, I'd hear my mom say. Fed up.

I knew it was about to start. I could never understand what triggered my mother's outbursts. Was it that my dad had come home late? Was it something that had been simmering for a while, something I knew nothing about?

My dad hunches down in his living room chair. My mom looms over him. He doesn't dare look up at her.

Fed up, my mom says. She spits these words out as if she were hammering home nails.

I'm fed up with your fooling around, Charlie. I tell you I've reached the end of my rope. God, I've reached it. I've had enough, Charlie. Had enough of you. And this God forsaken place.

She starts to reel around the room. The furies have her. She can't stay still. She's like an award-winning actress on a Broadway stage. Oh yes, my mom could be a drama queen. I won't say she didn't have reason.

My father hasn't moved. He hasn't said a word. And he doesn't. He just hunches down and lets my mom go on. He doesn't interrupt her monologue.

Having listened to them so many times, I wondered: does he think she'll just run out of steam? So many times I wanted to rush in and shake him, get him to stand up and say something, *anything*.

But he never does. His silence just riles my mother more. She's got her second wind. She's a whirling dervish.

I've had it, Charlie. Had it. I don't know why I let you drag me to this two-bit town. But I'm sick of it. And I'm sick of you. You and your drinking and the women you hang out with. You're a goddam tramp. I should have never married you, Charlie.

Maybe, in the end, my dad's silence works for him. My mom is crying now.

Charlie, I've got to get out of here. I feel like I'm going crazy, Charlie. I've been a good wife, better than you'll find anywhere . . .

When everything is said and done, my mom gives my dad the choice—divorce—or move.

We move. My dad quits his job and we take all our belongings and relocate to Victoria on Vancouver Island where my mom's brother, Pete, happens to be stationed with the Canadian Navy.

The only job my dad can find in Victoria is looking after a medium-sized apartment block. This isn't his cup of tea. But he'll do anything to keep my mom satisfied. He does what she tells him to.

Fortunately, for me, this gives my dad and me time to be together. My dad makes me toys. These are dolls made from colored yarn. My dad turns the yarn around and around one hand, then clips it. He ties a knot in the upper part of the yarn to make a head. And another for the waist. Another two knots tie off the legs. He spends hours constructing a cardboard house for the dolls that he's made.

Our first summer in Victoria is a scorching one. At the bottom of the steps leading to the basement my dad makes a swimming pool. He plugs the drain and runs a hose down. The water comes gushing out.

My dad sits on the step and talks to me as I splash in the water. It is a wonderful and lasting memory: the sunny day, my father carrying on his conversation, the coolness of the swimming pool in the summer heat.

My mom seems to like Victoria. She gets to dress to the nines. She entertains anyone and everyone who shows up at our apartment. My Uncle Pete brings by a lot of lady sailors. They're all dressed in their Navy uniforms. My mom loves it. She's the lady of the house. Would you like something cool to drink? And how about you? she asks. My mom dresses us both in expensive dresses. Where she gets the money, I'll never know.

But our time in Victoria doesn't last. Maybe it's because we're too poor. Maybe my dad isn't bringing in enough money. He applies and gets a job to work in a mine in Kimberly, in the Interior. But our stay there is short-lived. It's just a few months before my mom gives him another ultimatum. She's going back to the coast—with my dad—or without him.

My parents find a small one-bedroom suite on the west side of Vancouver. I end up sleeping on the couch. My dad has always been a drinker but now he's drunk more than he's sober. It gets worse between my mom and him. The arguments happen more and more often. My mom calls him lots of bad names. My dad doesn't stand up for himself. I wonder: maybe he believes everything she says is true.

My mom gets a job as a chambermaid in a high class hotel. It suits her: she can talk to all the big spenders. It's what she's wanted in her life, or needed: to pretend she's someone she isn't. She goes to work in high heels and beautiful clothes and make-up, in the hopes that some man will see her and take her away from the life she's leading. She doesn't have a good word to say about anyone. If anything, she's democratic: my mom criticizes everyone. It doesn't matter if they own a yacht or haven't a penny to their name.

My mom knows their every fault.

My dad gets a job in a butcher shop. When I'm about ten, my dad comes home one day from work and shows me his left hand: his fingers, wrapped in white bandages, are all the same length. The upper parts of three fingers are missing.

Gone, he laughs. All gone.

But there's a sharpness in his laugh I haven't heard before.

This marks the beginning of the end for him. My dad can't play the drums any more. My mom has him sell them.

What use are they? she tells him. Might as well get some money for them.

My dad spends more time in the bars with the friends that he drinks with. I see him less and less. Whenever he's home, my mom starts her tirade with him. He doesn't argue back. I'm learning quite quickly to be out of the house as much as possible. When I'm home, I'm sitting on the back step. When I'm not, I'm wandering the neighborhood trying to find a place where I can sit and forget what a sorry life we have.

Chapter Two

One summer my mom and I go back to Three Hills, Alberta, to see my mom's parents. Three Hills is in the Bible belt of Alberta and is well known for its Prairie Bible College. Although my grandparents are not religious, they love the community of Three Hills for the farmland and the rural style of life.

I call my grandfather Grandpa Blue Eyes. His eyes are so blue you can swim in them. My grandparents live in a log house and have several animals: cows, chickens and turkeys. Grandma has a big yard out back where she grows her own vegetables, everything a person needs: potatoes and zucchini, squash and pumpkins, along with beans and peas of every description and every kind of potato, from baking potatoes to the tiny little white ones that are so good with butter on them. What a summer it is! I play with the cows and chickens and help my grandma in the garden and pull carrots out of the earth and eat them raw.

Grandpa asks me if I want to go with him to the barn to

get the milk from the cows.

Looking at him, I ask, Milk from the cows?

Of course, how else?

How do you get milk from a cow?

From the bags.

Paper bags? I ask.

Grandpa thinks this is hilarious. I'm a city girl and I've never seen a cow, never mind a cow being milked. We head down to the barn. What an experience! I watch my grandfather, my eyes big as saucers and my mouth wide open. I have no idea that the milk is warm when it comes out. Grandpa's blue eyes are just twinkling. He is smiling from ear to ear.

From then on, every time we milk the cows, it takes us twice as much time because Grandpa and I break out into laughter. And then, we laugh some more.

I remember well the summer at Three Hills. I met so many people who were related to my mom and her family. My cousins took me horseback riding on a Clydesdale horse, a huge horse named Brownie. He had large brown eyes. His mane and tail were very short and he had a white blaze down the middle of his nose. I didn't stand even half way up his shoulders. I climbed a fence to get on him. But Brownie was very gentle. He just went where he wanted to go—despite my protests.

One early evening my grandma started covering all the mirrors in the house and the pictures on the walls with cloth. She said we were in store for a bad thunder and lightning storm. She explained that covering the mirrors and glass meant that the lightning would have nothing to see when it came near the house, and would pass on its way. She opened two windows and two doors. She told me that if lightning did hit the house it had to have a place to enter and another place to leave. Anyone hit by lightning, she said, was buried feet down, with their head out of the ground.

Now that scared me.

The storm came, and even though I had never been afraid of storms before, I was terrified. To this day, even though I know what lightning is, when it gets close, I get nervous. That night I remember the lightning coming out of the sky. It's forked lightning and I've never seen it before.

The sky is full of lightning and the house shakes with the thunder. I'm in tears.

There's nothing to be afraid of, my mother admonishes.

She laughs and laughs. My grandpa holds me close.

The next day dawns beautiful, sunny and warm, with the most beautiful blue sky. I've forgotten how afraid I was.

One Sunday we take a sightseeing tour of the surrounding countryside. There are my Uncle Ray and Uncle Pete, my mom, my grandpa and myself. We're speeding down a gravel road. I climb from the back seat of the car so that I can be up front with my Uncle Ray. For some reason, the door flies open, and out I fall. By the time the car stops, I'm up and running. My Uncle Ray runs towards me and picks me up in his arms. Blood is pouring down from my head.

When we arrive at the hospital, the doctor tells my mom, You've got one very lucky girl. She should be dead.

All I get are stitches. I don't even have a concussion. The doctors stitch up my head and I'm allowed to leave.

Uncle Ray is crying hard. He keeps saying I'm so lucky to be alive. He keeps hugging me so tight I can hardly breathe. Grandpa Blue Eyes seems in a state of shock. The doctors are more worried about him than me, as he is not a young man. My mom keeps saying to me, You'll be fine. I fall asleep in Uncle Ray's arms, with Grandpa Blue Eyes and Uncle Pete wiping my face and kissing me on the head and telling me that I'm so lucky.

When it comes time for the stitches to come out of the cut on the back of my head, my uncles and grandpa won't let Mom take me to the doctor in Three Hills. The three men take me instead. Uncle Ray and Uncle Pete and Grandpa Blue Eyes insist on coming into the surgery area. The doctor says that I'll be fine on my own. No, the three men say. They say I'm not going anywhere without them.

The doctor's office is small and even more cramped with three large men and a small redhead. The doctor tries to get them out. My uncles say if they have to leave the office they're taking me with them. The doctor finally gives in. I sit on Uncle Ray's lap while the sutures are taken out. Grandpa Blue Eyes wipes away my tears. In a few minutes, the procedure is over. The poor doctor is sweating. He's so glad that he's able to tell us we can leave. He tells me if I ever have to come back to see him, my uncles and my grandpa are going to have to stay home.

Goddammit, he says. They're worse to deal with than you are.

When we leave the doctor's office, Uncle Ray says the occasion calls for ice cream cones all around. So off we go to the ice cream shop. The shop is just down the street from the doctor's office. On the way, my feet never touch the ground. When my uncles are with me, I'm always in their arms. We arrive at the ice cream shop and Uncle Ray orders ice cream for all three of us. The ice cream is made from real cream.

I realize now that I was loved unconditionally by these three men, the three most important men in my life. At the time I did not know I would never see my Uncle Pete again.

He was killed not long after in a truck accident in Turner Valley, Alberta. Uncle Pete was on a trip there from Three Hills. He was following a truck loaded with long oil pipes and the truck stopped suddenly and the pickup that Uncle Pete was driving slammed into the back of the truck. The pipes came through the windshield and pinned him. He had no chance of escape.

Before leaving Three Hills, I went out one morning and surveyed the land in every direction. There was an expansiveness there which I have not experienced anywhere else. My grandparents' farm seemed to me apart from the world I knew. The abundance of my grandmother's garden and the care my grandmother gave to living things seemed unlike anything I had encountered in the world beyond the farm.

My mom decided before we went back to the coast that we would go to Creston, BC, to see my other aunt and uncle and cousins. They were rodeo people and had lots of horses and farm animals. We went by Greyhound bus.

My Uncle Joe and my cousins, Don and Woody, were typical cowboys with the boots and western shirts and the trophies for bucking horses and bull riding and all the things that the cowboys do in a rodeo. There was in the front corral a beautiful palomino stallion that my uncle and my cousins used for bare-back riding in the rodeos. The palomino was the colour of a copper penny. Its mane and tail were almost white. I was told he was part Arabian. I was warned by my uncle, aunt, and my cousins to stay away from him. He was a killer.

It was the wrong thing to tell me. When no one was around and I was bored, I would walk over to the corral and talk to him. It took him several days to trust me enough even to come close to me. One day, I went into the corral with him. I sat on the ground and patted his face and nose. I asked him what his name was. The name that came to me was Killer.

I said to him, You're no killer. That's not your way of life.

He nodded his head and we talked. I told him my story about the accident and my Uncles Pete and Ray and Grandpa Blue Eyes. At one point he kissed me. (He had a very rough tongue). And when he didn't agree with what I was saying, he would shake his head and his beautiful blonde mane and tail would quiver in the sunlight.

My uncle and cousins came around the corner. They froze on the spot.

What do you think you're doing? my uncle called out.

I'm talking to your horse, I said. And he's answering me.

My uncle said very quietly, Now you get up on your feet and very slowly you back yourself up to the fence.

I couldn't figure out why I should but I did as I was told. When I got to the fence, my uncle grabbed me and pulled me through to the other side. It must have startled Killer because he reared. My uncle's face was dead white. He shook me hard.

You could have been killed, he told me. Your angels must be looking after you.

My mom came out of the house. She looked at me and didn't say a word.

Although I never went into the corral again, I was at the corral many hours at a time after that. Whenever I came out of the house, Killer would come running over to the fence. He and I had some very long and wonderful conversations. I swear that he would never have hurt me. There was such a bond between us.

My uncle told me, That horse has no friends and listens to no one. He's totally wild.

But I didn't agree with him.

Grandpa Blue Eyes visited us in Creston. That summer he and I walked all over Creston; we travelled its hills and valleys. We sat by the water for hours and talked about all the wonderful things in the world.

Summer was coming to a close. It was the best summer of my growing up and I knew in my heart it would never happen again.

What I did not know was that I would see Grandpa Blue Eyes only one more time in my life. That was many years later. Soon enough I would find out love was scarce, if it was there at all.

Chapter Three

To my Grandpa Blue Eyes, you were—and still are to this day—the love of my life. I will never forget seeing you for the last time. You looked so tired. I hadn't realized that you had gotten old. But your beautiful blue eyes still sparkled when you saw me. We went walking down by the creek, holding hands.

We packed a picnic lunch and left my mother at the ranch with Woody and Don. Grandpa Blue Eyes and I set off across the fields and down the road. It seemed like going back to that time when I was small and Grandpa was drying the tears from my eyes.

We took our time and walked slowly because my grandpa was old and had a hard time walking. It took all my courage not to shed tears. It was a beautiful autumn day and the leaves were turning all different colours. Grandpa and I talked of many things, about the lightning storms, and just our love and caring for each other. When we finally got to the river bank, we found a spot under a tree and sat there and ate our lunch. It was like going back ten years.

We laughed and held hands. His hands were old and worn and rough from his hard life. But I didn't care; this was my wonderful Grandpa Blue Eyes. As the afternoon wore on, I noticed that Grandpa was getting more and more tired, so I gathered everything up and we started back to the farm just very slowly. I turned to my grandpa and I took him in my arms the way he used to hold me. I just held him tight and I told him over and over how much I loved him.

My grandpa took my hand and led me to a tree that had been knocked down. And he held me tight and told me he was going to die and it would not be long in coming. He asked me never to forget him and he said that he would always be with me.

Now, no more tears, he said.

And so we walked hand and hand slowly back to the farm.

Don and Woody wanted to know why we had been gone so long. We both said we were talking by the river and had just forgotten the time.

Grandpa excused himself and went to lie down before dinner. I went and got a coffee and went outside to the corral where my palomino horse had been many years before. I stood there with my coffee. It felt as though the horse of years ago was standing in the corral. He was there and he was talking to me and he was telling me not to worry, he would never leave.

My mother came outside and told me it was time for dinner. She saw the tears running down my face. She asked me why.

You will know soon enough, I told her.

Woody came out of the house and told me to sit down. I did. I knew what he was going to say. Woody looked at me sorrowfully and told me Grandpa was dead.

Woody said, The only reason he lasted this long was to see you again.

I want to see Grandpa Blue Eyes, I said.

Woody took me into Grandpa's bedroom. Grandpa Blue Eyes was lying on the bed peacefully, just as if he was asleep. I walked over to him and sat down beside him and took his hand in mine. It was already getting cold.

I sat there for a long time. When the doctor arrived, they asked me to leave Grandpa's side.

Grandpa Blue Eyes' funeral was three days later in Three Hills. He was laid to rest next to my grandma. I spoke at the funeral. Through the tears I told of my love for him and his love for me. Uncle Ray stood by my side and held my hand.

The Three Hills cemetery is on a hill overlooking green country fields and is well kept. After my grandpa's ceremony, Uncle Ray and I walked over to my Uncle Pete's grave site. I sat down on the grass between Uncle Pete's and Grandma's graves. I placed red roses on each grave site. More tears flowed as I told Uncle Pete how much I missed him and how much I wished he were there with me. When I looked up, I was alone. Uncle Ray had let me have this time to be with Uncle Pete.

It was time to leave the cemetery. I had no tears left, just the feeling of being alone in this world. Two of my favorite people no long existed except in my heart.

Our family decided to go out for dinner and be together. The fanciest restaurant in Three Hills was a step up from a diner. I sat beside Uncle Ray and held his hand. I was so quiet. I never said a word. That was different for me as I am not known for being quiet.

Uncle Ray took me in his arms and said very quietly so

that no one else could hear, Don't worry. I am not going to leave you for a very long time.

I looked up at him and smiled. We had our dinner and chatted some more.

The next day, without anyone knowing, I slipped away. Uncle Ray met me. We took a last trip to the cemetery to visit Grandpa and Uncle Pete and Grandma. It was a beautiful, sunny, warm day with just the hint of the wind blowing. When we got to the cemetery, it was very quiet. No one was there except the two of us. It was so peaceful. We had stopped to get ice cream cones and we sat on the grass between Grandpa's and Uncle Pete's site and we just talked. The sun was warm on us and the wind was blowing and you could hear the wheat blowing in the fields and smell the newly-mowed wheat and the grass and you could hear the odd sound of a cow mooing or a car traveling down the road. We sat there by ourselves for the better part of two hours and just talked and laughed. It was as if both Grandpa and Uncle Pete were there, joining in the conversation.

Finally, Uncle Ray said to me, It's time for you to understand. I know you wonder why I care so much about you. After all, you're my favorite niece.

Yes, I said, I had that feeling.

Well, he said, when you were born, I knew your mom and dad were having a lot of problems. I watched and when I couldn't stand it any longer, I came out to see you and your mom and dad. I wanted to take you home and look after you because I could see you were not going to have half a chance of a decent life. And I was correct. Your mom agreed with me but your dad said no. You were staying right were you were. I wanted to go to court to get consent to take you but I figured that would make your life worse in the end. So I just thought I'd watch from afar and just be there when you needed me. I will always be there when you need me, even if it is only to talk out a problem.

I sat there with tears streaming down my face.

I said, Uncle Ray, I love you so much. You have no idea how much what you've said means to me.

As we were leaving, I felt a sudden stillness and a total peace come over the cemetery.

Uncle Ray felt it, too.

He said, Uncle Pete and Grandpa know—they're here with us.

We walked back together to the car.

Uncle Ray and my mom and I went out for lunch before my mom and I left for Vancouver. When we were ready to board the bus, Uncle Ray took me aside and told me if I ever needed him, he was as close as the nearest telephone. I hugged him tight.

My mom was not being very nice to me. She kept pushing me towards the bus. We got on and I waved goodbye to Uncle Ray. The bus started to pull away. I tried not to show any tears but I noticed the tears on Uncle Ray's face. I pressed my face against the window and watched as Uncle Ray got smaller and smaller in the distance. As I turned around in my seat, my mom looked at me sternly.

What are you crying for? she asked. There's nothing in this world for you to cry about. So shut off the water works.

I looked out the window and saw the pastures and the fields of grain going by and the cows and horses in their fields.

One time when I looked out, I was sure I saw Grandpa Blue Eyes and Uncle Pete smiling at me through the window.

I shook my head and looked again. They were no longer there.

Chapter Four

My life was not a good one as I could do nothing right—not even hang the clothes on the line. I was not good enough for anything. That was made abundantly clear to me. Most days my mom came home from work and criticized me and called me stupid because I couldn't do anything correctly in her eyes.

I tried so hard to do everything I could to help her and make things a bit easier for us. I couldn't do the dishes correctly nor in fact hang the clothes on the line correctly nor fold clothes nor make the beds to her liking. The more I tried to help the more I got criticized for being stupid.

There were lots of days I just wanted to run away. But I didn't. I went to school in the west end of Vancouver. To me school was just some place to go to and hang out. At least, there my mom couldn't criticize me or yell at me. I never studied. Most of the time, I would just sit and daydream the time away. I remember lots of the time I would think about Three Hills and my uncles and Grandpa, wishing I could be there.

I resolved that as soon as I was able, I would get out of the house and go back to Three Hills to Uncle Ray. But that was never to be.

My teachers got a surprise every once in a while. Occasionally I got an " A" on my tests and the teachers were fast on my case to do some studying as they thought I had a very intelligent mind and the ability to go far in this life. I would just look at Mr. Bradley, who was my homeroom teacher, and say thank you. I figured my parents knew better than he did when it came to my abilities. Mr. Bradley tried hard to get through to me by having meetings with me after school and at recess. He kept trying to make me realize that I could be the top of my class with very little effort. The more he talked to me the more I shut him out of my world.

School at that time was a sad place for me to be. I had no real friends. I put up a wall around me. I would not take a chance on being hurt any more at school than I already had been at home. I was embarrassed about the way my mom and dad lived. I didn't want anyone to see us or come by to see how they argued. I joined no clubs nor participated in any school activities. I just kept to myself. It was easier to be on my own and be a loner than try to do otherwise. Sometimes I wonder how I kept my sanity. I would think of Grandpa and my uncles and the thought of them kept me sane.

When my mom and dad got into one of their terrible fights, I said, I'm going out. See you later.

I just wanted school holidays to hurry up and be over so that I could go back to school and hide out in the seclusion of the classroom.

Once, I overheard my mom talking to my Aunt Olla, who was married to my dad's brother.

Ray wanted to take Colleen when she was little, my mom said. I'm so sorry I didn't do it at the time.

I took off running before anyone knew I was there. I went for a long walk and I cried and cried. I found a telephone and called Uncle Ray in Calgary and said to him in tears, Now I understand what you were trying to tell me.

I could hear Uncle Ray taking a deep breath.

Calm down now, he said.

I told Uncle Ray that I had resolved I was going to move to Three Hills as soon as I could possibly pull it off. Uncle Ray told me not to do anything stupid and keep my chin up and remember that he loved me and when I needed him he would be there.

I love you Uncle Ray, I said. Don't leave me.

He promised he would not leave me for a very long time.

I had one girlfriend by the name of Delores. She was much like me—a loner and quiet. She also didn't care about school. She just went there to get out of being at home.

Delores was a lot taller than I was. She had long brown hair and green eyes. She came from a very poor family. I am not sure why we became friends. It might have been simply because her birthday was three days after mine.

One lunch hour Delores and I decided to go for a walk. She wanted to go down to the waterfront to look at the ships. We went down to the waterfront and were looking at the ships and we were dreaming of all the exotic places that the ships came from and thinking of the freedom that we both would have if we were traveling on one of them. It was a beautiful fall day, warm and sunny, just the kind of day to skip out of school and be with a friend and discuss and solve all the problems of our worlds.

We were walking along the dock at the foot of Georgia Street. There were a few warehouses there.

Look, Delores said, pointing. There's something there in the water.

I looked over the edge of the dock. That's when she pushed me. It was about twenty feet from the wharf to the water. I fell. At that time I could barely swim. There was a log beside the wharf, one so that the boats wouldn't hit the wharf and cause any damage. I just missed the log. Had I hit it, I would have been dead. But again, my angels must have been looking after me.

A tugboat came to my rescue. A man jumped into the water to be with me. I was crying and scared and choking from the water. The weight of my clothes and shoes kept pulling me down, but the man kept pulling me up so that I could breathe.

I was not hurt too bad. I had hurt my legs and my back when I hit the water and I was hospitalized for several days. Then I had to rest a lot. I listened to the radio and the World Series. The New York Yankees were playing and I was hoping they would win. And by the end of the series they did win the pennant.

My mom said now she had medical bills to pay—on top of everything else. I did tell her I took responsibility for not being in school. It was lunch hour and we were planning on being back in school that afternoon. It wasn't like we were planning on skipping out all day. Mind you, the thought had crossed our minds. But we knew our lives wouldn't be worth living if we did that. We had every intention on being back at school when lunch was over. I know Delores was sorry that it had happened. She apologized and I forgave her.

When I was fourteen, my life went from bad to worse. My parents split, finally. My mom got more demanding and harder and harder to live with.   All it seemed my mom was interested in doing was being dressed to the nines in hope that some of the high roller men at the hotel would give her presents or ask her out. She started trying to find a wealthy man to look after her. I only saw my mom after she came home from work and sometimes on the weekends. I lied about my age and I got a part time job waitressing at a restaurant, just to have a few dollars to help make our life a bit easier.

One Sunday afternoon, friends of my mom came for dinner. His name was Morrie and hers was Mary. They were an older couple. She had every disease known to mankind— or at least she thought she did. And she loved to talk about each one . . . Boring, I thought to myself. Martin tried to hit on me. I was fourteen and even at that age I knew enough to tell him to get lost. I guess he didn't expect that from a child because I never saw them again. Mom used to visit them regularly. But I refused to go. My mom got upset with me, but I never told her the reason why I didn't want to go. I just figured it was easier that way.

Chapter Five

One warm Sunday in April my mom and my Aunt Olla and I took the CPR ferry to Nanaimo on Vancouver Island and the bus up island to Qualicum Beach just for something to do for the day. I had never been on the ferry. I roamed the boat and the outside deck. I stood and watched the islands go by and the wake of the ferry as it ploughed through the water. The ocean water was green with a little bit of a white cap. I saw an occasional fish jump. I was thrilled. I even saw a whale in the distance.

During my travels in exploring the ferry, I noticed a young sailor, in his white cap and dark blue uniform. He was lanky, tall and thin looking. I noticed he had two differently coloured socks on. One was white and the other light blue. I was thinking how funny this was—two different coloured socks. Was he colour-blind or something? But I didn't pay much more attention. I was wandering about the ferry and enjoying the time to myself.

Everywhere I went on the ferry I kept seeing him. At one

point, he smiled and said hello. Being polite, I replied, and we started talking. He said he was on leave from Victoria, that he was stationed on one of the Navy ships. He said he was on his way back from Winnipeg, Manitoba, that his car had broken down in Montana, and he was heading back to his ship. His name was Jerry. He asked me my name and where I was headed. I told him that my mom and my aunt and I were going to Qualicum Beach for the day.

I was flattered that he would think of even talking to me. I mentioned that my Uncle Pete was in the Navy and gave the names of the ships he traveled on. Jerry said that he had gone out on the very same ships.

The more the two of us talked the more we seemed to have in common. Jerry suggested that he would like to come with us and see Qualicum Beach. I was surprised he wanted to join us, as he was heading back to his ship in Victoria. He bought himself a ticket for the bus. He got on and sat beside me and I introduced him to my mom and aunt. I told my mom and Aunt Olla about Jerry's car breaking down and that he was on his way to his ship in Victoria and that he was due back at his ship within the next three days.

The four of us chatted all the way to Qualicum Beach. When we got there and the bus had let us out, we went for coffee and something to eat at a restaurant. Jerry paid for all of us. I felt a mixture of shock and admiration. I was more than surprised that Jerry was spending time with us, and felt some admiration for how grown-up and responsible he was.

Qualicum Beach is a resort town with a long, sandy beach. It was April, and the sun was out but it was still chilly. The sky was beautiful and blue with white puffy clouds. I took off my shoes and socks and waded in the water with my coffee in my hand. Mom, Aunt Olla and Jerry gave me a bad time about walking in the water. They said I'd get my death of cold. I laughed at them.

Come on in, I shouted, the water's wonderful.

The beach went forever and the sand was warm from the sun. There were quite a few people walking on the beach, some with dogs and others on their own. I was proud of myself. I was about the only one with enough courage to walk in the water. It felt like heaven to me.

Afterwards, we visited some boutiques and antique shops. Jerry and I chattered almost non-stop the whole time. As we were getting on the bus to go back to Nanaimo, Jerry turned to my mom and aunt.

Would you mind if I came back to Vancouver with the three of you? he asked.

My mom hesitated for a moment. It was pretty obvious that Jerry had caught her off guard. She didn't know what to say.

I've had such a great time, Jerry said. I just don't want it to end.

Well, I guess I can't stop you, said my mother. But you've got to know you can't stay with us.

Jerry laughed. He said he hadn't any thought of doing so. He said he'd be looking for a hotel. He put all his attention on my mom.

I'd like your permission, he said, to visit you and Colleen, if you don't mind. Just for a couple days.

Well, my mom said, I could probably get you a room at the hotel where I work—and at a decent rate.

Mom made a couple of telephone calls and confirmed that there was a room at the downtown hotel where she worked.

So it was settled. The four of us chatted the whole time it took the bus to arrive in Vancouver. My mom asked Jerry a lot of questions. She asked him what he was working at and what he was planning to do in the future and what it was like being in the Navy.

I learned Jerry was almost twenty. He told us he was the baby of the family. When he was born, his mother was almost fifty. His father had died when he was fourteen. He said his sister had basically raised him from the time he was an infant and she was more his mother than his own.

My mom seemed to like Jerry from the start. He seemed so charming, in an awkward young man's kind of way. My mom couldn't do enough for him. She made dinner for the three of us and made the most of entertaining him.

As he promised, Jerry stayed in the hotel downtown. He and I walked all over the city, as though we were tourists, visiting the sights of the city. Many of them I had never been to. When Jerry brought me home, my mom would invite him in, and ask where we had been and what we had seen and Jerry's impressions of the city.

On the Sunday night, Jerry returned to Victoria to report to his ship. He was sailing on a three-month stint to Alaska and the Aleutians. After we had said our goodbyes, I thought that was probably the end of our friendship. As much as I had enjoyed the last three days, it seemed unlikely to me that I would ever see Jerry again.

Chapter Six

To my surprise I received letter after letter from Jerry during the three months he was away on his tour. He kept asking me if I loved him. I didn't know. After all, what is love to a fourteen-year-old? I thought it through as much as I could. Did I love him? I thought maybe I did. I remembered the three days we had been together. I had felt free—maybe for the first time in my life. I liked feeling that way.

I had never had a boyfriend before in my life. I answered every letter Jerry sent me, telling him of the bad time I was having at home. He told me of the loneliness of being far away from home on a cold drafty ship tossing about on rough seas. He told me he would be back in Victoria in early October and asked me if I would come over to visit him the weekend he returned.

I asked my mom if I could go. After all, I thought, I had my own job and my own money. My mom said there was no way I was going. Absolutely not.

Who do you think you are? she asked. Under no

conditions are you going to see anyone.

I got angry.

I am going, I said. And you're not going to stop me.

I had decided it was the one time in my life I was going to defy my mom. I had always been the doting quiet say-nothing girl. Up to that point in my life I had been invisible to most people in my world. I walked out on her.

I thought, When I come back from the island, if she does not want me back in the apartment, I'll go to Alberta to see Uncle Ray. He will be there for me. I know he will.

I took the CP ferry over to Victoria on the Friday after work. I had to rush away from work early. I was working now in the warehouse at a large department store downtown, stocking shelves and doing inventory.

It was a cold October night with the wind blowing and rain pelting down. By the time the ferry arrived at the depot in Sidney, I had gone through a hundred times what it would be like seeing Jerry again. I had butterflies in my stomach and a slight headache, but I thought that was probably from my not having eaten.

Jerry was the first person I saw when I arrived at the waiting area. He was wearing his Navy uniform. He was standing nonchalantly, his hands in his pockets. I came down the runway. His face brightened when he saw me. When I reached him, he took my hand.

How you doing? he asked.

Oh, cold! I said.

I'm so glad you're here, he said.

Me, too.

He put his arm around me.

The car's out here, he said. We'll get some coffee to warm you up.

That would be good, I said.

Jerry asked how my mom was. I had a lot of questions about his trip. I felt more awkward than I had ever felt and the questions seemed to help. We pulled into a coffee shop at Elk Lake. I called my cousin, Myrna. I had already asked her if I could stay at her house while I was in Victoria. She had grudgingly agreed.

I said that Jerry would stay on the base and that he would pick me up at Myrna's house each morning.

I don't have much room, Myrna said. You'll have to sleep on the couch.

I said that would be fine.

When we finished our coffee, Jerry drove down to the edge of the lake and parked. It was pouring rain. We sat talking for a long time. We talked about our separate lives and how we felt about them so far and what we really wanted for ourselves for the future. All Jerry could talk about was being married and having a wonderful house to come home to and a loving wife—all the things he had never had in his life. I said that sounded wonderful to me.

Jerry took out a small blue box from his jacket pocket. He opened it. Inside was the most beautiful diamond ring I had ever seen. I hadn't seen many in my life. I was in a state of shock. I knew what was coming. Jerry asked if I would marry him.

Neither of us had ever spoken of getting married. In my estimation, we were only friends. I sat beside him in absolute silence for what seemed an endless time and just looked at the ring. I knew Jerry was waiting for my reply.

What should I do? I asked Grandpa Blue Eyes.

The answer came back quickly: well, at least, you'll be free.

I thought of how I had been able to talk to Jerry and tell him my thoughts and feelings. I hadn't been afraid that he might ridicule me or call me dumb or stupid.

Yes, I said. I will marry you.

I felt on top of the world. My dreams had come true. Someone really did want me and did love me. I felt so lucky. Who would have guessed something like this could happen? I could hardly believe it. And, to think, in less than a week I would be turning fifteen.

It was quite a different matter when we got to Myrna's house and I shared the news with her. Myrna was a person who had little in the way of a sense of humour. She was a tall, imposing woman. When she opened the door to us, it was obvious from the look on her face she was only having me stay out of a sense of duty. After we had taken off our coats and were sitting in her living room, I told her the news of our engagement.

Getting married? she smirked. She eyed Jerry up and down, and then me.

Yes, I said.

I was still flushed from Jerry's proposal.

You're just kids. You're too wet behind the ears to even think about getting married.

I know what I'm getting into, I said.

It didn't matter to me what Myrna might think. I kept looking at the diamond ring on my finger. It sparkled with so many possibilities, so many promises. The light from it seemed to fill the room.

When I had a few free minutes, I called Uncle Ray and I told him the news. For the first time in my life he yelled at me. I started crying.

Uncle Ray, I said, it's a way of me getting out of the house and away from my mom and a chance for her to live the life she's always wanted.

Uncle Ray made me promise if anything went wrong, I would call him immediately and he would be there to take me away.   He also reminded me that I was as much a daughter to him as his real daughters. I promised to call him if anything went wrong, but I vowed that I was going to do everything in my power to make my marriage work.

Jerry took me around Victoria the next day and introduced me to some of his Navy friends. I felt flattered to meet them. I met Colin Woods. Jerry had asked Colin to be his best man. Colin and I got along from the second we were introduced. He had a wonderful sense of humor and everyone laughed at the things he said. He took me aside and told me I was far too young to be thinking of marriage.

You haven't even begun to live yet, he said.

I said I knew what I was doing and that I was happy to know him and have him as a friend. I told him I would be looking forward to seeing him at the wedding in January.

I got back to Vancouver early Sunday. I wondered how I was going to tell my mom about my engagement. I expected there would be a fight and that I would have to say I was set on going ahead with the marriage despite what my mother thought.

Myrna had already called my mom. I had just gotten in the door of our apartment when my mom cornered me.

You pregnant? she asked.

No, I said. I am definitely not.

When you getting married? she asked.

I said we had thought of having the wedding in January.

My mom didn't seem upset.

Don't expect any help from me, she said. Whatever it costs, you'll have to pay for it on your own.

As we had planned, Jerry came over the next weekend to

help prepare for the wedding. I was surprised how sweet my mom was to him. With Jerry, she seemed to want to show off her best. She made the two of them drinks and asked Jerry questions over dinner. It was a side to her I hadn't seen much of, not since the days when my Uncle Pete used to bring by his sailor friends. She sure hadn't done anything like that for me. Oh well, I thought, it'll be great. At least, they get along. And just maybe I'll have a family for the first time in my life.

We decided to get married on the last Friday night in January. It was going to be a simple wedding at a United Church in the west end of Vancouver, with just six of us altogether. That was fine with me. I didn't want a big wedding. I just wanted it done so I could be free of my mom and start my new life.

Jerry sailed again for another two-month tour to San Diego. He was gone about three weeks when I got a telephone call that he was in the hospital at the Navy base. He had arthritis to such a degree he couldn't walk. Immediately, I took the ferry to Victoria to visit him at the hospital. He was in pretty rough shape. Jerry lay in bed, unable to move without pain. Even the slightest movement was excruciatingly painful.

Well, I thought, this is the end of our marriage. He won't want to marry me now that he's so ill. He will probably want to get out of the service and go back to his home town of Winnipeg.

I was wrong. Jerry was more determined than ever to get out of the hospital. I stayed with him as much as I could over the weekend. I stayed at Myrna's house. Either she would drive me out to the hospital or I would take the bus out to see Jerry. I had to go back to Vancouver on the Sunday so that I could be back at work again on Monday morning.

The doctors confirmed Jerry had arthritis. They said that Jerry was surprisingly young to have this disease. Jerry was feeling better under the doctors' care. His symptoms had lessened. He asked me if I still wanted to get married.

Of course, I do, I said. Do you?

He answered that he did.

The doctors kept Jerry in the hospital for about a month and then started him on his rehabilitation. I went over every weekend to see him. On the third weekend he phoned me. He told me he had a pass from the hospital and that he would pick me up at the ferry. When I came off, I ran to him. We held each other in a long embrace and kissed again and again.

Soon Christmas was upon us and Jerry came from Victoria to spend Christmas and New Year's with us in our one-room suite. It was cramped with just the three of us. There were barely enough chairs for all of us to sit down.

It was a sad Christmas. My dad was not invited to our house. There wasn't a tree or any decorations. I'd offered to buy a few things to cheer the place up but my mom had refused. Jerry gave me a Christmas card: that was all. I was disappointed. I had bought my mom a cameo and matching earrings. She didn't put them on, just put them aside. I'd gotten Jerry a new shirt. He said it was wonderful. He put it on; it was light blue, the same colour as his eyes. I thought I had done well. I had bought my dad a card and some aftershave in case he visited.

One evening between Christmas and New Year's my mom had my dad over to the apartment. The reason for her doing so was that my dad's signature was needed for me to get married. When the doorbell rang, I couldn't believe the person at the door was my dad. His shirt and trousers were torn, and dirty. He smelled of sweat and liquor. He was hardly able to string two words together. He was smaller, more fragile, than I had remembered him; it was as if something inside him was broken.

I thought, I'm going to cry. If I did, I knew my mom would be furious. I didn't need the wrath of my mom at this point in time.

I held back my tears. I was saddened by the sight of my dad. At the same time, I was angry that he had let himself decline to such a state.

My mom paid hardly any attention to him. She acted as if my dad wasn't there. She put the marriage form down on the kitchen table.

Sign it, she said.

She could have been easily talking to the wall.

Here, Dad.

I showed him where to put his signature.

He took the pen and pressed it to the paper. The signature was illegible. It didn't matter.

Now, you've got to go, my mom said.

My dad didn't reply. He made his way slowly to the door. I followed him outside. On the step I asked him if he would come to my wedding and give me away.

No, he said. I don't think so.

Couldn't you come? I pleaded.

Your mom doesn't want me there, he said. She told me to stay away.

I started to cry.

I'm so sorry, Dad, I said. Will you come to Victoria and see us after we're settled?

Sure, sure, I will, he said.

And he turned to leave. He went down the stairs slowly,

the way an old man might. I watched him walk down the street until he disappeared. He never looked back.

At that moment, my heart felt as though it was about to break. Somehow I knew I would not be seeing my dad again. Somehow I knew this was the last time.

Chapter Seven

Jerry went back to work in Victoria and I stayed with my mom. The ladies at Mom's work threw a bridal shower for me. They gave me a set of sheets and some towels and a few odds and ends for my kitchen. That was what I started my married life with. All of it fit into a suitcase and I had lots of room to spare.

I know my mom was glad to get rid of me. She could hardly wait to get me out of the house. We hardly talked to each other any more. That was fine with me because I had determined in my own mind that my new life would be so much better.

Jerry and I were married in the office of the church in the west end of Vancouver. The office was small. There was a large desk and several chairs. The six of us, including the minister, barely fit.

My wedding dress was white. It was a dress a girl might wear to graduation or out for a night on the town. Jerry was dressed in uniform. The best man was supposed to be

Jerry's friend, Colin, but he had just left on a three-month tour. The elevator operator at my mom's work said he would fill in. I barely knew him and Jerry had never met him. My bridesmaid was a girl from school. The best man was drunk before he arrived at the wedding ceremony. There were no flowers. My mom complained loudly that she didn't have a corsage to wear. I gave Jerry some money and he ran to a nearby flower shop to get her one.

The ceremony was about ten minutes long. After a round of congratulations, we all walked back to my mom's place for something to eat. We had cold cuts and buns. There wasn't a wedding cake, not even a cookie. My cousin, Mike, showed up at my mom's place in time to have a few drinks. Mike was in his Navy uniform. He had a short brush cut. I remember thinking his eyes were as blue as Grandpa's. Mike told me where he was stationed and that if I needed help to call him any time. He told me he had heard via the grapevine that Jerry's reputation was not the greatest. I did not want to believe what I was hearing. I promised him if I needed help I would call him.

I was tired and my nerves were ready to break. I could hardly wait to get out of the house. I changed into a dark skirt and blouse and threw on my coat and I was ready to leave. I left my white dress lying on the bed.

When my mother came in and saw the dress, she asked, What do you want me to do with it?

Sell it, I said. I don't really care. You can give it away.

I really didn't want to keep it any longer. I didn't want any reminders of the wedding.

The time came for us to leave for the ferry to the island. Jerry and I picked up our suitcases and walked the sixteen blocks to the terminal. The CPR Princess ferry was sailing at midnight. When it was time, we boarded. Jerry and I had a chance now to talk on our own. I told him that someday I wanted to have a proper wedding. Jerry agreed with me. He said that if he known what the wedding was going to be like, he would have had me come to Victoria and we would have gotten married there. We could have had the ceremony at the chapel on the base. It would have been fancier and all of his friends could have attended. I agreed with him. But it didn't matter now. It was enough that we were legally married.

When we arrived in Victoria the next morning, the day was cold and gray. Jerry had rented a furnished apartment for us. We had a two-mile walk to get to it. We stumbled along, the suitcases in our hands. It was a long, cold walk and the suitcases were heavy. By the time we arrived, I was exhausted.

The apartment was on the top floor of a three-story walk-up. When we opened the door, I thought I had died and gone to heaven. It was twice the size of my mom's place in Vancouver. It had a kitchen with a refrigerator and stove, and a decent-sized living room. It lacked a bedroom, but a Murphy bed pulled out of one of the living room closets. The front windows looked out onto the street. I pictured us sitting in our living room and watching the world go by.

That night we had the apartment full of guests, all of Jerry's friends, people I had never met before. Luckily, they brought food and something to drink. I had a rum and coke. I had never drunk any alcohol to this point in my life. I thought it was fine. It tasted sweet. By the end of the night most of Jerry's friends were drunk or well on their way.

On Monday Jerry went back to work for the first time as a married man. I cleaned up the apartment. I wanted to be the best wife I could be.

My husband. What wonderful words they were. I was

free at last! I didn't have anyone to answer to except my husband. Oh, how I loved him. And now my mom was free, too. She could do whatever she wanted and with whomever she liked. I hoped she would find someone and start leading the life she wanted for herself.

I expected Jerry to arrive home from work around five o'clock. But five o'clock came and went. By seven o'clock I was worried and upset and pacing up and down the apartment. When the door finally opened and Jerry arrived home, he was drunk. He apologized for being late. If we'd had a telephone, he would have been able to call. Without one there had been no way for him to reach me. He told me his friends had taken him to the Tudor House, a local pub, to celebrate his getting married. One drink had followed another. He said that each time he had tried to grab his hat and attaché and make it to the door, his friends had taken his belongings and hidden them.

Jerry had just lain down on the couch when there was pounding at the door. I opened it and all of Jerry's friends came pouring in. They were all drunk. They got Jerry up and proclaimed that he and I had to go with them. We had to help explain their absence to their wives. Otherwise, they'd be in trouble. Off we went, all these drunken service men and myself in tow, to prove to their wives that Jerry and I, in fact, had gotten married.

Surprisingly, their wives were not mad at them at all. They were happy to join the party and have some fun, as well. The women were a lot older than I, in their twenties. Ann, one of the wives, took me aside and told me I shouldn't be surprised. This was how the end of the day often turned out. She advised me that I would soon get used to this kind of life. Of course, I agreed. But, in my heart, I thought of my dad. I hoped that Jerry wouldn't go the same way. I didn't know if I could handle all the drinking.

We ended up at Pete and Joanne Prince's basement suite. It was small, much smaller than Jerry's and my place. With ten people in it, it really was cramped. But we had a good time. The guys got drunker. I had a rum and coke. I was not a drinker and really did not like it very much or how it made me feel.

Jerry and I arrived home at two o'clock in the morning. Jerry had to be back on the base for work by seven o'clock; otherwise, he'd be disciplined. I was told the usual punishment for being late was not being able to return home for a week. Jerry had no choice but to be on time. He was still drunk when he left for work on Tuesday morning.

I started looking for a job almost immediately. Unfortunately, I was only fifteen and not very many companies wanted to hire a fifteen-year-old married woman. I tried to get a job, but to no avail. We were able to get by on Jerry's meager salary. We managed to afford a telephone. I learned to cook, not well, but I did learn. We were lucky in that a lot of Jerry's friends would invite us to their places for dinner on weekends. It always turned out to be a drunk. I stuck to my one rum and coke for the evening. Consequently, I did most of the hostessing but I didn't care. It was fine with me. I just watched what was going on and laughed when I was supposed to laugh.

I had a secret, though, one I didn't tell to anyone. I knew I had made a mistake getting married. Sometimes I stared across the dinner table at Jerry and wondered what in the world I had done. Anyone looking in might have thought we were getting along. Jerry would talk about his day at work, and some of the things that had happened there. And I would do much the same, though I had less to tell. After that, we didn't have much else to say.

Some nights we would go down to the corner of Yates and Douglas, which was known as Pussers' Corner, and we'd sit and watch all the people going by. At home we filled the silence between us by having other people over. Or we'd go out with Jerry's friends. Jerry liked talking with his buddies, and the wives seemed to enjoy taking me under their wing.

Sex was a disappointment. I couldn't believe that so much was made of it. It didn't take very long, and I wondered why in the world women did it. It wasn't very enjoyable. When the other wives talked about the times they had in the bedroom, I blushed. I couldn't believe what they said. They told me that sex was meant to be enjoyed, and that I needed to get Jerry to change his ways. I brought the subject up to Jerry a number of times. I said that I wanted our love life to be different. I was quite passionate in my own way. But Jerry didn't respond to me. And he said the things I had heard were dirty and he wasn't about to do anything like that. I resigned myself to the life we had. I hoped that something might change to make it different but I had no idea what that might be.

When I look back, I suspect that Jerry felt much the same as I did: getting married had been a mistake. We hardly knew each other. Jerry must have wondered how he had gotten into such a predicament. How many times he must have wondered how to get out of it. As it was, we never talked about our marriage. We just carried on. I was adamant I was going to make our marriage work, no matter what. After all, what other choices did I have? I was fifteen. I had no education to speak of. I didn't have a job, or any training. And I had nowhere to go.

As for Jerry, I suspect he resigned himself to the same fate as I did. We'd made a bad decision, but it was one we were going to have to live with. There was no going back. I thought that just maybe if I worked hard enough, things would get better. Maybe Jerry and I could have a life together if we tried.

Chapter Eight

One Saturday evening in the first month of our marriage, Jerry answered the telephone. From what I heard Jerry say, I could tell it was a call from my mom. A few minutes later, Jerry hung up the phone. I looked at him. I could see he didn't know what to say.

It's my dad, isn't it? I said.

Yeah, it is, said Jerry.

My mom had called to say that my dad had died. His body had been found under the Cambie Street bridge. He had been homeless. Cambie Bridge was where he had slept at night. The cause of his death was pneumonia.

In my mind I went over all the things my dad and I had missed out on. I thought about the last time we had seen each other. I remembered the moments we had spent together when I was a child, although there were not many. I remembered the swimming pool he had made for me in the heat of summer and the time he had made me wool dolls when I had nothing else.

I got myself prepared to leave for the funeral in Vancouver. I pleaded with Jerry to go with me.

I don't want to face this alone, I explained.

There's no way I can go, Jerry said. I can't get leave.

Won't you ask? I said. I need you to be there, Jerry. I don't think I've got the strength to do it alone.

There's no use me asking, said Jerry.

Please, wouldn't you?

You don't know how these things work, Colleen. By the time I get my okay, the funeral will be over.

Maybe, if you asked, I said.

Jerry said, Colleen, I know you can handle it.

On the day of the funeral, the sky was grey, and it was raining. The funeral was held in the Catholic Church downtown. The service was a very simple one. I brought a bouquet of red roses with me to the chapel.

My mom and I sat together. There were only ten people at the service. I was surprised that some of the street people whom my dad had gotten to know came to the funeral. It helped me a lot to know that people who were poor (they slept under the Cambie Street bridge) cared enough about my dad to be there.

The service was at the back of the church. I was given to understand that if you were not a churchgoer your funeral was held there. The plain casket was closed. I don't know how my dad was dressed.

The actual service was less than thirty minutes. A young man stood up and spoke about my dad. He was also a street person from under the Cambie Bridge. He spoke very eloquently of how much my dad was liked. He said my dad was a person who cared deeply about others. He recalled the occasions when my dad shared food or something to drink with others. I sat there crying, thinking about my dad and his life.

My mom leaned over.

What are you crying about? she asked. Your dad was just a bum.

I didn't answer her. I didn't dare. If I had, I would have screamed at her. She seemed oblivious to what I might be feeling.

She was telling me about a time my dad had come to her place for food. He had been sick then.

I kicked him out, she said with satisfaction.

I looked at my mom with a feeling of disgust.

I told him I didn't have anything for him to eat, she said.

I couldn't understand how she could talk this way about a man she once loved and cared about and with whom she had lived so many years.

Did you really dislike him that much? I asked. You couldn't have offered him a sandwich or a cup of coffee?

I would have thrown out food rather than give it to your father, she said bitterly. He was a good-for-nothing all his life.

You must have loved him once, I said. You married him. You liked him enough to have me.

That was a long time ago, she said. I'm sorry I married him. He was below my social standard. I was sorry I had you. You were always in my way. I met lots of very rich men, but as soon as they found out I had a daughter, they wanted nothing more to do with me.

I sat crestfallen. Why was I surprised? I had always known in my heart how my mom had felt.

The service ended. The casket was lifted up.

Then and there, I made a promise that I would never turn a hungry person from my door. If anyone came to my house hungry, I would give them my last piece of bread. And it is a rule I live by to this day.

Chapter Nine

While I was at my father's funeral, I was so sick I couldn't keep anything down. I thought it was nerves from dealing with my dad's death. I could barely keep down a drink of water.

When I arrived back in Victoria, Jerry said I had better see a doctor. I had started to lose weight. Along with this, I was tired all the time. I could barely put one foot in front of the other. I snapped at everyone, including Jerry, and had no patience whatsoever. The doctor told me I was pregnant. The baby would arrive before my sixteenth birthday.

Jerry seemed happy about this. I hadn't had a clue about my pregnancy. I wasn't even sure how a baby was delivered. My mom had never told me a thing. The doctor put me on a prescription as I was so dehydrated and so tired. He threatened that unless I took time off to recuperate, he was going to put me in the hospital for a few days to rest. I promised I would take it easy and get lots of bed rest. I told him that maybe my symptoms were worse because my dad had just died. He asked me to see him weekly for the next two months. He said I was in danger of losing my baby since I was so run down, and that he wanted to make sure I took good care of myself.

Jerry wasn't thrilled at the news that I wasn't to do anything, but for the most part he kept quiet about it. One morning I kept throwing up, and there was blood. The doctor put me in the hospital for three days. I came out of the hospital under strict orders to take it easy.

The summer rolled on and I lived on purple grape popsicles. I just loved them. They were my one treat. By the time autumn came, I was so big it was hard for me to get around. I didn't go out of the apartment much. I made myself take a walk each day and to try to keep healthy. I hadn't gained much weight, only fifteen pounds. But I felt so big.

My mom did not take the news of my pregnancy well. She told no one.

I went into labor and Jerry took me to the hospital. After many hours the baby was born. We named her Sarah. She was a beautiful child with dark hair and the most beautiful blue eyes. I loved her the minute I saw her. Sarah weighed just over seven pounds and was twenty-one inches long.

Sarah was a very quiet baby and barely ever cried except when she was wet or hungry. I sat for hours just looking at her and holding her. My mom did not come over to Victoria to see her new granddaughter. My cousin, Myrna, came once. That was all that I saw of her for a long time.

There were no flowers at the hospital. When I arrived home, the apartment looked the same as when I had left. There were no flowers there either. Not even a card from my husband.

During the summer before Sarah was born, Jerry had

taken over managing the apartment block. Jerry wasn't paid but it meant that we got our apartment for free. There was a lot of work involved. The apartment was in the basement of the building and did not have much light. It did have a bedroom, though. And, because it was free, we were able to save some money.

We took care of the building and collected the rent from all the tenants at the end of each month.   It was hard work, but we didn't mind.

One day, when Sarah was only about a month old, Jerry arranged for one of his friends, Jimmy, to baby-sit while we went out for dinner. Oh, what a nice treat. I showed Jimmy where the diapers were drying. I hadn't folded them and put them away but they were clean and warm. I also showed him where the bottles were kept and explained what time Sarah would be expecting to be fed. I left the name of the restaurant and the time we expected to be home. Then off we went.

The restaurant wasn't very expensive because we couldn't afford very much. But it was very nice just to be alone with Jerry for a few hours. We were able to sit and talk. I was still too young to have a drink in a restaurant. But that was fine. I was not much of a drinker. I enjoyed being waited on. It made me feel like I was someone.

We left the restaurant around ten and arrived home. Jimmy greeted us at the door, but it wasn't the kind of greeting I expected. Jimmy started upbraiding me for not having left any diapers or a bottle of milk for Sarah. I was surprised by Jimmy's outburst and I was angry. I told Jimmy I didn't know what he was talking about. I reminded him that before Jerry and I had left, I had shown him where the diapers and the bottles were kept. Jimmy didn't answer me. He grabbed the money Jerry offered him and made for the door. Sarah was wet and hungry. After I changed her diapers and gave her a bottle, she seemed quite happy. She didn't seem any worse for the experience.

I spent most of my time helping Jerry with the apartment block. I swept the floors of the building twice a day and the front entrance. Sometimes we took calls from tenants who had complaints. Jerry would have to go and check on a leaking faucet or collect back rent. Meanwhile, I tried to be the best mother I could be.

Often Jerry's best friend, Colin, would help me with the chores around the building when he had time off. Colin was a very stocky man, all two hundred pounds of him, and a gentle soul. He was the centre of any get-together. He had a joyful laugh that rang throughout any room he was in. He cut quite a figure in his uniform.

Colin was to have been best man at our wedding. But his ship had sailed two days before we were to be married. Colin and Jerry had been in training together in communications. Colin had the reputation of chasing women, the typical single sailor with a girl in every port. He loved Sarah and often joined Jerry and myself in our walks around the neighborhood with her. We three adults were like the three musketeers. Sometimes, when Jerry was at work, Colin and I would take the baby and walk down to the park.

Our first Christmas as a married couple with a baby, we did not have very much. We bought a few things for Sarah. We were able to afford a turkey and, thanks to my cousin, Myrna, and a few of our friends, who showed me how, I was able to make my first turkey dinner, with all the trimmings.

Jerry was not allowed to do too much because of his arthritis. As a result, he was permanently assigned land duty. By this time, I had found out I was pregnant again. I was expecting our second child. I was sixteen.

One afternoon in early January I answered a knock at the door. I thought it must be one of the building's tenants. When I opened the door, it was an older woman whom I didn't recognize. She had another woman with her. From the look of them I thought maybe they were canvassers from a church. The first woman took out a card and handed it to me. She said she was from child welfare. She said their office had gotten a complaint about me. They had been told I'd been neglecting my child.

I stood stock still. I didn't have the words to respond.

Could we come in? the woman asked.

Of course, I said.

The two of them came in and stood in the hallway. One of them asked me where the baby was. I showed them. Sarah lay fast asleep in her crib.

The woman who was the first to speak to me handed me a piece of paper. She said because of the complaint they'd received they were apprehending my child.

No, I screamed at her. You can't.

The second woman pushed past me, picked Sarah up, blankets and all, and hurried past me. Sarah was still sleeping. The woman who had done most of the talking said I was to call and make an appointment to speak to them later.

Then they were gone. I was alone.

I tried to phone Jerry but was unable to locate him. I tried to reach Colin. There was no answer. By the time Jerry arrived home, I was half crazy, and sobbing. I kept asking myself who would have done this and what could possibly have been their reason.

Jerry was calm. What had happened didn't seem to bother him. He made no attempt to hold me or put his arms around me. I couldn't understand why he was acting so detached.

His words were even more surprising.

Pull yourself together, he said. It's not the end of the world. It'll be fine. After all, you're pregnant. You're going to have another one.

I was inconsolable. I knew Jerry was wrong. Losing Sarah was the end of my world. I don't know how I got through the next few days. I spoke to my mom on the phone but she didn't have very much to say. I called Myrna.

You can't fight the welfare, she warned. You can try. But you won't win.

Thank heavens for Colin. While Jerry seemed aloof and uncaring, Colin was willing to listen. We went out walking for hours. I cried and cried. I felt totally alone in the world. With each day, I was less and less able to cope. Yes, life went on. But to me it felt like death. I kept asking myself, Why? What had I done wrong?

I made an appointment to go to welfare. I asked Jerry to come with me. He told me he was too busy. Colin offered to come with me to the meeting.

Colin and I arrived at the welfare office. I was scared. I was close to throwing up. Colin put his arm around me. My name was called.

A woman took us into her office.

Who are you? she asked Colin.

He's a friend, I said.

This is a private matter, she said to me. I need to see you alone.

Go ahead, Colin said to me. I'll be out here when you're done.

I was trying hard not to cry, trying not to show any emotion. The woman motioned me towards a chair. The first question I asked was: how was Sarah? The worker said she was doing fine and that Sarah was in a good home. I asked her when I was going to get Sarah back. She answered that Sarah couldn't be in my care while I was under investigation.

Investigation? I said. For what?

For neglecting your baby, she said.

I would never neglect anyone or anything, I screamed at her.

The woman seemed unimpressed. I asked if a doctor had looked at Sarah.

Yes, she said.

I asked if the doctor had found anything wrong with Sarah.

No, the woman answered. Sarah seems in good health.

So, why am I being investigated? I asked.

There's been a complaint. We're obligated to look into it, she said.

I started to cry. It was all too much for me to understand. The office door opened and Colin walked in. He put his arms around me. I cried and cried. Then, the worker asked me a question I could not believe. She asked whether Sarah was my husband's baby—or Colin's.

Colin swore at her.

We're out of here, he said.

The woman seemed nonplussed.

You can make an appointment, she said, for a month from today. And next time, bring your husband—or come alone.

She gave a Colin a disdainful look. Colin and I left the office and went for a walk.

I'm so sorry for the way that woman treated you, I said.

Don't worry about it, Colin said. I have to tell you: I wish I was Sarah's father.

Really?

I'd be a better father than Jerry will ever be. Jerry doesn't deserve you. You're too good for him.

He's my husband.

But you don't love him, do you?

I didn't reply. I respected Colin and cared for him deeply but not as a lover or husband.

I was married and I respected my marriage vows. In my world, when you married, you married for life.

As the days went by, Jerry appeared indifferent to the hurt and loss that I was feeling. There wasn't an hour that went by I didn't think of Sarah. I wondered where she was and if she was being cared for and if someone loved her the way I did.

Jerry seemed to find reasons to be away a lot of the time. He would go out to have a drink with his buddies. I wasn't invited, as I had been before. I felt he was ashamed of me, that he didn't want to be seen with me. Colin, on the other hand, came by often and helped a lot by talking to me and listening. I poured my heart out to him.

The appointment with welfare was coming up and I was scared. My nerves were on edge. During one of my visits to the doctor, he advised me to take it easy. If I didn't, there was a chance I could lose the new baby.

Colin came with me to the doctor's on most of my visits. Once, the doctor asked me where my husband was. I said he was working and wasn't able to come. The doctor called Colin into his office and spoke to him alone, while I waited. I found out later he had told Colin that losing the baby remained a real possibility.

Colin admitted that he cared a lot for me. But he also knew where I stood in terms of a relationship with him. The doctor had suggested I would need Colin's support since my husband wasn't available. He cautioned Colin not to allow me to go to the welfare worker's office on my own.

When Colin came out of the doctor's office, I asked him

what he and the doctor had been talking about.

Nothing, he said. Nothing you have to worry about.

He smiled. I felt relieved. If Colin wasn't worried, there was less reason for me to be concerned.

The day before my appointment with the welfare worker, I asked Colin over. I was going to ask Jerry to come with me the next day. I thought it would be helpful if Colin was at our apartment. I thought Jerry would be more open to the invitation if Colin was there.

Jerry refused. He said he was sure I could take care of the meeting myself.

In that case, Colin said, if you don't mind, I'll go with Colleen.

Go ahead, said Jerry, if you're so interested. But I have things to do.

He walked out of the room. To me it seemed Jerry didn't care what was going to happen to myself and Sarah.

Colin picked me up the next day. Jerry had already gone out without saying anything to me. When Colin and I arrived at the welfare office, I was called in by the same woman I had spoken to before. Colin got up with me. The woman informed Colin that since he wasn't a member of the family, he was excluded from the meeting. Colin kept on standing. He was tall and he was big. He said firmly that I wasn't attending the meeting on my own, took my arm and ushered me into the office.

The first thing I asked was: how was Sarah? The woman said that Sarah was fine and doing well.

When am I getting her back? I asked.

I wasn't prepared for the answer I received. The woman said that their office had applied for temporary guardianship of Sarah and that a year's guardianship had been granted.

Sarah won't be going home, she said. You'll be given supervised visits every three months. Visits are fifteen minutes long.

I turned to Colin and started to cry.

What have I ever done to anyone to deserve this? I asked.

Colin didn't answer. He held me while I cried. I don't know what Colin said to the worker. But the next thing I knew she stood up. She told us it was time that we left.

She directed her words to me.

Next time, you'd better come without your friend. He is not to put one foot in this building. I'll get a restraining order if I have to.

Her eyes were blazing.

Colin and I got up and walked out. Outside the office, I told Colin I was in terrible pain. It was my back. Immediately, Colin got me to the car and we drove to my doctor's office. My doctor assured me that I wasn't in labor but said that the stress wasn't doing me any good. I had to relax or else I was going to find myself in trouble. Under such circumstances, the chance of the baby surviving was very small.

I could see that Colin was still seething from our visit to the worker. I had never seen him so upset.

Are you okay? I asked.

Yeah, he said. How about you?

Still a little shaky, I said.

You're probably starving. I'll take you to lunch.

Over lunch we talked a long time. Colin said that he knew I respected my marriage vows. He said that he respected me for that. He promised he would be by my side for as long as I wanted him there.

I really appreciate your help, I said. But this is my battle and somehow I have to solve it. I just hope I have the strength for it.

This is one person, he said, who's not going to abandon you.

I breathed a little more easily. I was going to make sure I didn't lose this baby. Having Colin there was going to make things easier.

It was almost time for me to go home and make dinner. I asked Colin if he wanted to come over. He said he didn't think he would. He said that I had to talk to Jerry and make him understand the seriousness of what was happening. He dropped me off at home and told me to call him later.

I opened the door of the apartment. It was so quiet. I felt afraid. I wanted to turn around and run. I settled myself down. I kept thinking I had to do what was best for the new baby. I started making Jerry's dinner.

Jerry arrived at six. He sat down at the table to eat. He asked me how the meeting had gone. I told him. I said that welfare had guardianship of Sarah for a year, that we had supervised visits and how these would happen. I said I had seen the doctor and that the doctor had warned me that I was on the verge of losing the baby.

Don't worry, Jerry laughed. Everything'll be fine. You'll be able to take care of it.

I stared at him. I wondered how he could talk like that about his child and wife. I couldn't reply.

When Jerry finished his dinner, he said he was going out, that he'd be back in a couple of hours. I asked where he was going and what he was doing. He ignored my questions. He picked up his jacket, and walked out the door.

I thought, He thinks it's my fault. He thinks I'm to blame.

I felt terribly alone. Was there anyone I could talk to?

I decided not to call Colin. He had done so much for me already. I thought I'd call my mom. Maybe she would understand what was happening. On the phone, my mom had very little to say. I told her what had been decided about Sarah, and that I wasn't going to get her back, and that Jerry didn't seem to care one way or another. She heard me out. I knew she didn't care either.

You made your bed, she said. Now you lie in it.

I hung up, angry, and crying. Really, what else had I expected?

I called Myrna. I asked her what I could do. Was there any way she knew that I could get Sarah back?

You'll just have to wait and see how things turn out, she said.

I listened for Jerry to come home. When I heard his step, I met him at the door.

We have to talk, I said. I really need your help, Jerry.

Well, Colleen, I'm here, aren't I? he said.

He seemed faintly amused.

Yes, I said. But what about Sarah?

Don't worry about her, he said. She's being looked after. Enough about this. It's late and we're both tired.

Our conversation was over. I wondered what more I might do. All I knew was I felt more alone than I had ever felt before.

Chapter Ten

Several weeks went by. During that time, Colin phoned and said he was leaving for a three-month cruise. He said he would be back home around the time the baby was born. I was to look after myself, he said, and to bite my tongue when I went to meet with welfare. He reminded me that it wouldn't help to get upset. I promised I'd be careful about what I said. I told him to have fun chasing the ladies. I phoned the welfare office and made an appointment for my visit with Sarah.

The next day I arrived at the welfare office at about two in the afternoon. I was ushered into the office by a tall, matronly lady with lightly graying hair. We sat down. I said I needed to know the charges against me. She opened a file that lay on her desk.

That's clear enough, she said. You're considered in neglect of your child. It's fairly simple, isn't it?

You've got to prove it, I said, defiantly. I haven't been

charged, have I?

No, she replied. There are no charges against you.

Then, I'd like to see the complaint, I said. I want to know who made it.

I can't do that, she said. That information is confidential.

I didn't know what more to say.

I said, I want to see my daughter.

I was shown into the next room. There was a nurse in a white uniform and a child with her. It was Sarah. I rushed over to her and took her in my arms. She was so excited to see me.

I held her tight and cried. I told her how much I missed her and that I loved her. I sang a lullaby to her, the one I sang to her every day.

The fifteen minutes were up before I knew it. The nurse separated us. Poor Sarah started crying. She raised her arms for me to pick her up. The nurse lifted her up and walked out of the room.

Meanwhile, the worker had reappeared. I pleaded with her now.

What do I need to do to get my baby back? I asked.

She didn't answer my question.

She said, You'll get to see her again in another month. In the meantime, don't get your hopes up.

Why not? I said. I'll do anything. I want my daughter back.

You're not getting her back, the woman retorted. You can call in three weeks for your next appointment.

Yes, I said.

I had lost any courage I'd had. I remembered what Colin had advised about biting my tongue and being careful about what I said. As I left the office, I resolved I'd jump through any hoops to get Sarah back. No matter what was required of me, I would do it without question.

When Jerry came home that night, I told him about my visit with Sarah and what I had resolved to do. He didn't say anything.

Later that evening, Colin called from Hawaii. He said hi to both of us and asked how everything was. I told him about my visit with the social worker. He said he would call in a week or two when he got a chance. The next stop on his way home was San Diego. He would try to call from there.

The next two visits to the welfare office were in the spring. The last one was just before the new baby was to be born. My visits with Sarah left me feeling hopeless. Poor Sarah. When it was time for me to leave, it was hard for her to say goodbye. Sarah held her hands out to me. And the woman took her away.

After I left the welfare office, I walked and walked. I was in tears. I hurt and I was angry. Where—and to whom—could I turn?

When Jerry came home that night, I tried to talk to him. But he was non-committal and skipped over the subject. I couldn't reach Colin because he was unavailable. His trip had been extended and he wouldn't be back in Victoria for another four months. I wrote Colin a letter and told him what was happening.

His reply came several weeks later. He said once he got home he would see what he could do to help.

The next month Jerry and I gave notice and we moved to a duplex in an area of Victoria called Esquimalt. It was a two-bedroom duplex and had its own yard. I liked it because we were able to sit outside and enjoy the warm weather.

The chance of getting Sarah back seemed less and less likely to me. Each time I visited, the welfare worker said I would have to prove myself before I could get Sarah back. I started feeling that I would never have her back again. It hurt deep inside me. It took all my strength just to get through each day.

One spring morning I went into labor. Jerry rushed me to the hospital. After a long labor, I delivered a boy. He was thin and small, with reddish hair, beautiful blue eyes and long fingers and toes. I named him Colin Jerry, after the two men in my life.

I had had a bad pregnancy and a very hard labor. It was two weeks before we were released from the hospital. Little Colin was a very good baby. In the mornings when the weather was warm, I would put him in his carriage and I would sit with him in the yard. He would sleep in the fresh air and warm sunshine.

In the meantime, Colin had returned from his trip. He was thrilled that the baby was named after him. He loved the baby. Whenever he visited, he brought toys and diapers. The baby looked like Jerry more than anyone. But Jerry seemed indifferent. He didn't pay much attention to the baby at all.

Still, Jerry seemed happier. Some weekends we hired a baby-sitter for a few hours and went out for a few drinks and to socialize. Jerry was on guard duty at the base and often had to leave at midnight for work. Colin would take me home. I understood there were rumors about us. I ignored them as best I could. After all, none of them were true. I would never cheat on my husband. The thought had never even crossed my mind.

One morning that spring I was sitting in the yard with the baby. He was asleep in his carriage. A car drove up. It was a car I didn't recognize. Sarah's worker got out of the car. She came into the yard.

Are you here to give me Sarah back? I asked expectantly.

I've done everything you've asked me to.

No, I'm not, she said.

If you're not here to bring Sarah back, then why are you here?

I'm here to take the baby.

I screamed at her. No. You can't.

My screaming woke the baby. He started to cry.

Why are you doing this to me? I asked.

The worker said she was responding to a complaint that the baby was outside crying all the time.

That isn't true, I told her. Not for a minute is it true.

I was crying hysterically.

Another woman got out of the car. She came over and picked the baby up in her arms. The welfare woman told me to come and see her the next morning. The two walked back to the car with Colin, got in, and drove away. Colin was barely a month old.

I was distraught. I knew I hadn't done anything wrong. I hadn't neglected anyone. How could someone have said that of me? What in the world had I done to deserve being accused in this way? I was young. But I wasn't a bad mother. These thoughts and questions kept running through my head.

Colin was on another trip again so I couldn't reach him. When Jerry came home that night, I hardly spoke to him. I told him that welfare had come and taken the baby. Jerry seemed unconcerned. He said it wasn't a problem. I asked him if he would take the next day off and come to welfare with me. He said no. He said he had to work. This part, he insisted, was up to me to take care of. I couldn't understand his refusal. I couldn't understand how he could seem so indifferent.

I didn't sleep that night. I paced the house. I cried and

cried. In the middle of the night, I called my mom. She hung up on me.

I called Myrna.

Oh well, she said. There's not much can you do.

The next day, after Jerry left for work, I got myself ready with a heavy heart and drove down to the welfare office. I have no idea how I got there. I don't remember driving. I waited in the office. The welfare woman asked me to come in.

What's going on? I asked her. Who in the world is doing this to me? Who's saying these things about me?

I can't tell you, the worker said. The information about the complaint is private and confidential.

What do I have to do to get my children back? I asked

The worker wouldn't answer the question. She said I could see my children once a month for fifteen minutes in her office—and her office only. I wouldn't be allowed to be alone with them.

Am I being charged with anything? I asked.

No, the worker said.

If I'm not being charged, why can't I have my children back?

You can't have them back, she said. Just accept it.

When Jerry came home that night, he didn't ask about the baby or Sarah or what welfare had said. He announced that he was leaving for a three-month tour starting the next day. He said he would be in contact with me either by phone or letter. Otherwise, he would see me when he got back.

I couldn't believe what he was telling me.

How can you leave like this, Jerry? What am I supposed to do?

What am I supposed to do? he replied. This is my work. I don't have a choice, Colleen.

The next morning I drove Jerry to his ship. Afterwards, I went to the beach, found a place to sit, and watched the ships sail out of the harbour. I sat and cried. It was a warm, sunny day and the sea was calm. I stayed sitting there until it was afternoon. I thought about my children. I couldn't understand the reasons I had lost them. I thought about the way Jerry had been acting. I didn't understand him at all. Colin had disappeared from my life. I had tried to reach him several times but there had been no reply.

I was alone.

As I was sitting and thinking, a young woman with reddish hair like mine sat down not far away from me. She could see how upset I was. She introduced herself. Her name was Anna Pine and she was a Navy wife, too. She said I didn't look too good. I admitted I didn't feel very well. She asked me how old I was and I told her. She asked me how long I'd been married. I told her two years. She sat down beside me and put her arms around me and said not to worry, everything would be fine.

He'll be home soon, she said.

She asked me if I'd join her for a cup of coffee. I said I would like that a lot. We found a coffee shop. We talked and talked but I didn't tell her about my children or mention what I was going through. She just thought I was very young and just married and that I was missing my husband. Anna had a husband who was on the same ship as Jerry. Her husband's name was Calvin Pine and he was in the same department as Jerry. Calvin was next in charge after Jerry. Anna and Calvin already had children. She was quite a bit older than I was.

The next days were hard for me. I was alone in the apartment. I decided I had better get out. It was doing me no good to stay in and do nothing. I went down to Eaton's department store and applied for a job and got one in sales. I started the job but I kept mainly to myself and made few friends. I was hurting from the loss of Sarah and the baby. I didn't want to tell anyone what had happened. I felt ashamed. I didn't want anyone close to me. I had been hurt enough.

Spring turned into summer. I never heard from Colin. I wondered what had happened. Colin had said he would always be a friend. I had tried his number but it was no longer in service. I missed him terribly. What had led him to drop our friendship? I wondered.

I had letters from Jerry and a few phone calls. He asked how I was and told me what he was doing. In the meantime, Anna and I were getting to know each other. When she brought her kids over to visit, I made sure Sarah's and the baby's things were put away. I wasn't ready to tell Anna about my loss.

I went back to the welfare office for my appointed visit. It was wonderful to see Sarah and Colin again. Sarah, especially, had grown so much. I held both of them close to me. I begged the welfare woman to let me have them back.

They're permanent wards of the court now, she said. They'll be raised together by the same family.

This piece of news broke my heart.

How can you make this decision, I asked, without us agreeing to it?

Your consent isn't required, she replied. It's a matter of applying to the court for permanent guardianship, and getting it.

How can you do this? I asked. I haven't been charged. There's no proof I've been neglectful.

She looked at me with disdain.

Our conversation is over, she said. You can come and see me in a month.

As I was leaving, the worker informed me that permanent guardianship meant that my visiting privileges were revoked.

You won't be seeing your children again, she said.

I won't?

It's in their best interest. There's nothing to be gained by prolonging matters any further.

How can you do this? I asked.

The worker didn't reply. She showed me out of the office and said goodbye.

Jerry called that night and I told him what had happened. Sarah and the baby wouldn't be coming home. We wouldn't be seeing them again.

Well, he said, it's for the good of everyone.

I couldn't believe what he was saying.

Don't you care? I asked.

Look, he said, haltingly. Colleen, I've got to go now.

He hung up the phone.

I had missed my period. I knew this wasn't unusual given the stress I had been experiencing in the past while. I went to see Dr. Morris. He told me I was six weeks pregnant. At the news, I broke down in tears. I told him that I wanted to leave my husband but that, if I did, I would have no chance of getting my babies back.

I can't handle this any more, I cried. I don't want to lose any more babies.

Dr. Morris assured me I would not be losing this baby. He said he would help me through all of the pregnancy and after, too.

Jerry phoned the next night and I told him the news. He didn't say very much. It was hard for me to know how he felt about it. I had so many different feelings about it myself. Feelings of sadness and loss, then happiness, were all mixed together.

The next day I told Anna that I was pregnant. She told me she had suspected that I was pregnant but she hadn't wanted to say anything. She got a baby-sitter that night and we went out for dinner and celebrated. Sarah and the baby were never far from my thoughts.

I received a telephone call from Dr. Morris the next day. He told me that tests had confirmed that I was expecting. He told me I had to quit work. Otherwise, I was in jeopardy of losing the baby. I went into work that afternoon and gave my notice.

The next Saturday was the day Jerry and Cal were returning. It was a beautiful day, hot and sunny with very little breeze. It was a glorious summer day, so still. Anna and I arranged to meet early that morning at the rock where we had first met. We sat and watched the ships come in. There were five destroyers in the convoy and they looked absolutely stunning as they appeared over the horizon and slowly got larger. We sat and watched them as they came into the harbor. Anna and I got up then and drove to the dock.

There were a lot of other wives and lovers and children on the jetty with flags and balloons everywhere. The band was playing brightly, and loudly. The band's brass trumpets shone in the bright sunlight. There was so much excitement in the air, and so much laughter. It was wonderful to see the ships as they came in succession into the harbor. The ship that Jerry was on was the last one in harbour. She required her own jetty as she was the largest in the convoy.

Anna and I stood side by side waiting for our husbands to come off ship. Cal came off first and Anna and he embraced.

Anna introduced us to each other. Then Jerry came off the ship. He hugged me tight and gave me a long kiss. He took my hand and told me he was so glad to be home.

Jerry told me that he and Cal were only home for the weekend. Their ship was sailing again on Monday, for a five-day cruise. He told me he would be back home on the following Friday, and then he would stay at home for a couple months. I was so glad to see Jerry. Maybe, just maybe, I thought, we could put all the sadness that had happened behind us.

Anna and I agreed we would meet for coffee the Monday morning after the men had left. Jerry and I said goodbye to Anna and Cal, and went home. Jerry seemed happy to be home, and was very loving.

I brought up the subject of how I was feeling about the loss of Sarah and the baby. Jerry avoided talking about it as much as possible. I thought it might be better not to force the issue since Jerry was leaving in two days. We stayed in that night. I tried to keep the conversation light. We went to bed early and made love. As I fell to sleep, I felt a ray of hope. Maybe everything would turn out all right, after all.

Jerry and I got up early Sunday morning. Jerry got a call from one of his friends. They wanted to get together with us for coffee. I wanted to spend the precious time we had left to be alone with Jerry. But Jerry felt differently. He wanted us to be with his friends more than he wanted to be with me. At least, that was what came into my head, but I tried to shut it out.

Why didn't I grab my suitcase then and there and walk out? I was angry enough to. But where would I go? And hadn't I made a promise to do all I could as a wife? I was determined to show my mom I could make this marriage work, despite her opinion to the contrary. I would prove her wrong. I would be a good wife. And I would prove welfare wrong. I was a good mother.

At six Monday morning I drove Jerry to work and said goodbye to him. The day was dreary. A sad rain was drizzling down. Anna and I met for coffee. I wasn't feeling very well. We cut our coffee time short. I had a doctor's appointment for blood tests later that morning and in the afternoon I had my visit to the welfare office.

I went to the doctor's first. I had to wait for a long time. After Dr. Morris examined me, he confirmed I was in good health.

Just take it easy, he said, and try not to do anything strenuous.

He said that, as far as he could tell, this baby was going to be large. He would see me in two weeks.

I had about two hours before my appointment at the welfare office. I decided to go downtown and look in the shops. It was raining hard. I was tired. And I was worried, wondering what welfare would want me to do next.

When I got to the welfare office, the worker I had spoken to at the previous meeting surprised me by saying that Sarah and Colin were in the next room and that I would be able to see them. She told me this would be my last visit with them. I started to cry. The worker said I must promise not to cry in front of the baby and Sarah since any tears would upset them unnecessarily.

I got myself settled and I went in to see them. How they responded when they saw me broke my heart. Neither of them wanted anything to do with me. They would not even come to me when I called their names. When I got near them, they both began to cry. I asked the worker why they were so different with me.

It's because you're not their mother any more, she said. They have a mother now who loves them and takes good care of them.

I ran out of the office, sobbing. I sat in my car for a very long time and cried. In my heart I knew I didn't have any fight left. Welfare had won.

The next day I received a telephone call from the welfare worker. She wanted to make sure I understood that Colin and Sarah were permanent wards and reminded me that I would not be seeing them again.

Doesn't there need to be a hearing first? I asked.

Yes, the worker said. It's already been held.

Why wasn't I told? I asked.

You didn't have to be told, she replied.

She said the hearing had been held *ex parte* and that meant I had no part in it.

When I got off the phone, I felt my world had fallen in. I went to Colin and Sarah's room and sat there alone. I felt myself leave. I was in another world. It was a world that was peaceful and quiet and one that accepted me. It was a world where there was no loss or hurt. It was a world where you didn't have to prove anything to anyone. It was a world that loved you.

It was nothing like the world I knew.

Chapter Eleven

Jerry came home and we settled in for the arrival of the new baby. I kept off my feet as much as possible.

One morning we got a knock at the door. Jerry went to answer. It was Jerry's mother, his sister, Jean, and her husband, Henry. They had just arrived in town from Winnipeg. Jerry was as surprised as I was to see them. He welcomed them in with open arms. I had never met any of them before, not even Jerry's mom, Jessica. She was a severe-looking woman, with a pinched mouth, and not much in the way of compliments. It became very clear to me that Jessica did not have a very high opinion of me. She looked around the apartment as if it was beneath her to be there.

Jean was a stocky, dark-haired woman, and she deferred to every opinion that Jerry gave. You could tell that Jerry could do no wrong in her eyes. I had the distinct impression that she felt I was not good enough for her younger brother. Both she and Jessica smiled at me the way you might to a child.

I was nervous. I was trying to put on a good front for Jerry's family but I knew I was failing miserably. That made me even more nervous. I poured coffee and tea and tried not to spill anything. I couldn't say a word. I just sat listening to the conversation and poured when the cups needed filling.

Jerry's family stayed for the day. Jean had the habit of washing her hands after touching anything. That was unnerving for me. I thought she felt that the house was not clean enough. I looked at the floor. I looked at the couch and coffee table. They seemed clean to me.

We went out for dinner. By this time, I had rallied enough courage to attempt to contribute to the conversation. But, every time I said something, it was as though Jessica and Jean didn't understand what I was saying. I could have been speaking a foreign language as far as I could tell. They ignored whatever I said except when Jerry asked me a question or brought me into the conversation.

I was glad when it came time for Jerry's family to leave. It was late. Jerry invited them to stay overnight; they declined the invitation. I was very glad that they did. I didn't know whether I could have stood them any longer.

Jessica asked about the baby and Sarah. Jerry said that for the time being the children were being cared for by someone else. He said we had decided that we needed some help with Colin and Sarah. Jerry said they would be coming home soon.

I was ashamed of Jerry for lying. I started to say that things weren't quite the way Jerry was saying. Jerry gave me a stern look. I stopped and bit my tongue. With Jerry lying to Jessica and Jean's questions, there was not very much I could say. I kept my mouth shut.

After Jerry's family left, Jerry was angry with me. He said I was a poor hostess and that I should have been more hospitable. I should have called his mother "Mom". I asked how I could have been any more welcoming when I knew, for a fact, that his family didn't like me. I said the only reason his mom and sister had stooped to talk to me was because I was his wife. I said it was obvious they didn't think I was good enough for them.

You know, I said, maybe I am not good enough for them. And maybe I'm not good enough for you. Maybe you want me to pack my suitcase and leave because I really feel that's what you want me to do.

Jerry said I was being stupid again.

I said, No, it's true, Jerry. I'd have to be royalty to please your family.

Jerry took me in his arms and said that wasn't true. He said he loved me very much.

He said he was looking forward to the baby. He said maybe we would have better luck with this child. I relaxed in Jerry's arms. But I wasn't convinced. I asked myself, Could I really believe what Jerry was saying after everything that had happened?

The summer was hot and I was ready to have the baby but I was tired and not feeling well. I stopped seeing Anna and anyone else, for that matter, and stayed close to home. I talked on the phone for hours with Dr. Morris. He had a plan to make sure I didn't lose this baby to welfare. Once the baby was born, the baby and I were to see him once a week. That way, his visits with me could be written down in a diary he would keep.

I had told Dr. Morris I didn't think I could handle another round with welfare. He agreed. He suggested I call the welfare office and set up an appointment to see the worker.

Maybe I would be allowed to see Colin and Sarah before the new baby was born.

I did as he suggested. I called the welfare office and spoke to the worker. She said that the children were fine and both doing well. She said that Colin was crawling and sitting up. Sarah was now potty-trained. She said Sarah was a wonderful little girl and had long, blonde hair. I asked if it would be possible to see them. The worker said no. It would be hard for everyone concerned. There was a large lump in my throat. I just said good-bye, and thank you. I wanted instead to say thank you—for nothing. But I thought better of it and held my tongue.

When I got off the telephone, I started to cry. No matter what I said, welfare would always have the last word. I felt defeated, bruised, and sick at heart.

Jerry had been away for five days on maneuvers and was returning that afternoon. I had promised him I would meet him when he arrived. It was still two hours before the ship docked. I decided I would drive down to my favorite spot to watch the ships come in. It was a beautiful day. The sea was calm. I could see fish leaping out of the water. Near the shore there was a seal swimming. He seemed to be playing. He would dive and come back up a little further along and then turn back again in the opposite direction. As his head came up out of the water, he looked around. What a lucky seal you are, I thought. To be able to play and enjoy life so much. I wondered what it would be like to be a child and have fun. I figured in my short life I had not had much enjoyment. I wondered if it could have been any different. I felt I had missed so much.

As I sat and watched the seal, I saw the ships come into sight. They were lined abreast and looked, on one hand, very formidable, and, on the other, very beautiful. I watched as the ships came closer and maneuvered into harbor. As the last ship turned in, I saw it was Jerry's. She was the largest and the most impressive of the ships.

I really didn't want to leave. I had felt some peace there for a while. For a short time I'd had a rest from my problems.

I got in the car and drove down to meet the ship. As I was waiting for Jerry to disembark, I saw Anna. We chatted for a few minutes. She scolded me for not calling her and coming over. She said we could, at least, have gotten together for coffee. I promised her I would come and see her the next week—that is, if the baby hadn't already arrived.

Jerry came off the ship. I put on a brave face. I had made a pact with myself I would not tell him that I had heard from welfare. He kissed me and held me close.

Jerry told me that he was going to be home for the next three months.

I said that was good.

Maybe, I thought, we could start living like a family again. I told Jerry that my cousin, Mike, had called. Mike had just moved to the west coast. He was working as a stoker on a submarine and had just arrived in Victoria. I said I was looking forward to all of us spending some time together.

I don't think so, said Jerry.

I was surprised.

Why not? I asked him incredulously.

I don't like him, Jerry said. I don't want you seeing Mike, or his wife. They just want to meddle in our affairs.

I protested.

I will see them, I said.

Besides my mom and Myrna, Mike was the only other member of my family. Jerry relented a little. He said if I had them to the house, I could only do so when he was not at home. I felt down-hearted and confused. It seemed to me that Jerry was being unnecessarily difficult.

On Friday night of that week I went into labor. Jerry took me to the hospital. When it was time, Dr. Morris attended. He told me not to worry. I was going to get through this. And this was a child I was going to keep. His words of support made me feel stronger.

Arlene Belinda was born with blue eyes and strawberry-blonde hair. Her hair was so thin and wispy it was as if it wasn't there. She was long and thin for a baby, with long fingers and toes. Jerry and I had compromised on her name. I liked the name Arlene, and Jerry had wanted the baby to be named Belinda.

Dr. Morris kept me in the hospital for two weeks. I had gotten an infection and it had to be cleared up before I went home. Arlene, as we called the baby, was a delight, with a very calm nature. Dr. Morris came at least twice a day to see me and the baby. He spent hours talking with me. The other mothers in the room wondered why he was there so much. I didn't tell them.

Once I was out of hospital, I took Arlene to see Doctor Morris once a week. I had lost any confidence I had felt caring for Colin and Sarah. I was scared now. I was terrified I might do something wrong. I was afraid of any mistake I might make.

The day came when Dr. Morris released us from hospital. He told me not to worry. He said he was on my side.

He said, Go home, Colleen. And enjoy your daughter.

Jerry picked us up. At home Anna and Cal had left flowers and a present for Arlene. My cousin, Mike, had also sent flowers and a card. Jerry had not got me anything. Again, I took a deep breath and bit my tongue. I had learned to do that a lot lately.

One day Anna took me aside and asked why I didn't take Arlene and move out on my own. She said Jerry didn't treat me very well.

What do you mean? I asked.

It's pretty obvious, she said. He doesn't care about you.

I said I couldn't leave Jerry. My wedding vows said "for better or for worse". I still believed in that.

Besides, I said, I have no place to go, no money—and a new baby. I've thought a lot about leaving but for now I can't.

I gave her a hug.

She said, Just let me know if you need anything.

At home, I was enjoying Arlene so much. She was a wonderful baby. Dr. Morris said he was proud of me. He said he could see that Arlene and I had formed a strong bond. Dr. Morris said I could breathe more easily now and start to enjoy life.

No one can take Arlene away now, he said.

I said, Thank you for all you've done for us.

I felt I had finally turned a corner in my life.

Chapter Twelve

Jerry's ship had finished being refitted and was ready for sea trials. Jerry was going to Long Beach, California and then to San Diego on a cruise. He would be away for three months. I had just found out I was two months pregnant. I was seventeen.

I took Arlene down to see her dad off. We waved good-bye as the ships put out to sea. I took Arlene to my favorite spot to watch the ships leave the harbor. They looked as formidable and as beautiful as ever. I told Arlene to wave to her daddy. He was on the ship, I told her. Maybe he would see her and wave back.

Arlene and I went home to start our life together without Jerry. A month later I got a telephone call from Jerry. He asked if I felt like coming down to spend a few days in Long Beach with him. I was excited. I had never traveled so far, and I had never been to California.

Jerry said he had arranged for his friends to babysit Arlene for ten days. His friend, Vic, worked in the same department as Jerry; his wife's name was Denise. I had never met them before. Jerry told me to take Arlene's food and clothes to their house and explained that I would have to pay them.

I asked Dr. Morris what he thought of the idea and he said it was a good one. He thought the trip would be a wonderful opportunity for me to relax. He said I should visit Vic and Denise with Arlene and see how she got along with them. He suggested that if Arlene was comfortable with them, I could then make the arrangements. He told me to leave a letter with them with his name and phone number, and my written permission allowing him to treat Arlene in the event of a medical emergency. I went home and made the arrangements.

Vic and Denise were a young couple, but older than Jerry and myself, with no children of their own. Vic said I should bring over Arlene's crib and her clothes. I paid Vic in advance, gave the number where I could be reached in Long Beach, and Dr. Morris' number. I kissed Arlene goodbye. Denise said not to worry. She said they would take good care of Arlene and to have a good time.

I was excited when I got on the bus for Long Beach. Everything had fallen into place, with so little effort. An older lady sitting next to me on the bus asked where I was going. I said I was going on a holiday. I was going to visit my husband where he was stationed in California.

When I arrived, Jerry was at the bus terminal to meet me. He had arranged a hotel for us to stay at. He took me to the play land at Long Beach. It had the highest roller coaster in the world and there were plenty of rides. It was a wonderful place, right beside the Pacific Ocean. I loved every minute being there. The following days Jerry took me around the city. We went out to restaurants and talked. When Jerry went to work, I was free to wander the city.

The day I was to leave, Jerry brought me to the bus station. As I was about to get on the bus, Jerry said he had bad news. He had received a call from Victoria. Vic and Denise had taken Arlene to the welfare office. They had told the office that I had abandoned Arlene. She was now in welfare's care.

When I heard Jerry's words, it was as though a knife went into me. I didn't feel it. I didn't cry. I stepped up into the bus. I didn't say good-bye to Jerry. It was as if he didn't exist. My only thought was Arlene.

It was early afternoon when I arrived home. I got my car and I drove immediately to the social worker's office. I demanded to speak to the worker. She took me into her office.

I said, I want Arlene back. I want her back right now.

The worker said, She's already been placed. She's now a ward of the court.

How can you possibly do this? I said.

You abandoned her.

I did no such thing. I paid those people to look after Arlene.

I told her that I had given Vic and Denise the phone number in Long Beach where I could be reached. I said I had given them Dr. Morris' telephone number in case of any emergency.

The worker said Vic and Denise had reported that I had left Arlene with them for a few hours but hadn't returned for her.

That's not true, I said. It isn't true at all.

I'm just telling you, the worker said, what was reported to us.

The worker said Arlene was now a ward of the court.

I asked if I could see Arlene.

No, you can't, said the worker.

I walked out. I went straight to Dr. Morris' office. By this time, I was hysterical. When I saw Dr. Morris, I broke down.

Who is doing this to me? I asked. Who hates me so much that they're doing this? I've never hurt anybody.

Dr. Morris spent at least two hours talking to me. He gave me two pills to take when I got home. He said they would help calm me down.

At home, the house was empty of anything of Arlene's. I had brought all her clothes, toys and her quilt to Vic and Denise's when I had left. I had two photos of her and these I placed beside me as I lay down to sleep. I prayed that she was in good keeping. I wondered where in the world she might be, and with whom. Maybe it was because of the pills I had taken but I could not cry any more. I felt nothing. It was as if there was nothing left of me to feel. I had a body but it was a shell inhabited by someone I didn't know. Eventually, sleep came. It was a relief. I would not have to think, or remember.

The next day I could hardly move from my bed. I couldn't raise my head. I wanted to die. That was what I wanted more than anything.

Later in the day the phone rang. I stumbled over and picked it up. I heard Dr. Morris' voice.

He said, Colleen?

Yes? I said.

I didn't recognize the sound of my voice. It sounded hollow. I put down the phone. The next thing I remember there was a knock at the door. I got up to answer it. My legs were heavy as if there were weights on them.

I opened the door. It was Dr. Morris. He took me by the

shoulders and shook me very hard.

He said, Colleen, listen. You need to fight—and to fight hard. You need your wits about you now.

He asked me who my best friend was.

Anna, I answered.

What's her phone number? he asked.

I showed him a list of numbers I kept on the wall by the phone. He picked up the phone.

Anna arrived soon. Dr. Morris told me to take a shower and get myself dressed. When I came out, I found Dr. Morris, Anna and my cousin, Mike, together. Anna said she had made some coffee and to come into the kitchen. I wondered where Mike's wife was. There was a brass nameplate on the kitchen counter. It seemed strange to me that it was there. It had a number and the name of Mike's boat. Anna was crying.

Get your things, she said to me. You're not staying here by yourself.

I want to stay here, I said.

No, you're not, said Dr. Morris. You're going to stay with Anna for a couple days. Just until you get your strength back.

I'm going to get to the bottom of this, said Mike. Something about this stinks like rotten fish.

Yes, something does, said Dr. Morris.

Who in their right mind would do this? Anna cried. You're a good mother.

At Anna's words, all my feelings of rage and desperation suddenly surfaced. I started to cry uncontrollably. My body was wracked by waves of sobbing. Anna held me.

I thought, All these years I've tried to be a good person. I've jumped through every hoop. I've tried and I'm tired of it. Tired of being accused. Tired of having to prove myself.

Mike said, I'm going to put an end to this as soon as I can.

How? I asked.

Colleen, you've got to stop feeling sorry for yourself, Mike said.

You're right, I said. I have my children to think of.

Never mind your kids, he said. You've got to start thinking about you, Colleen. You're a strong person. You've come this far. Now you have to go the rest of the way.

I'll do that, I said. I promise.

Anna picked up my suitcase.

Let's go, she said.

Of the days that followed, I don't remember much. I remember that I no longer wanted to live. Anna made me meals and talked to me, really nursing me as best she could. I could hardly put one foot in front of the other. I plodded to the table when called and tried to eat but couldn't keep anything down. I lived simply from one moment to the next. I felt someone was plotting against me. At times I thought it was Jerry, sometimes I thought it might be Dr. Morris. I doubted that. But I was obsessed and haunted by questions. Why had this happened? And, who was responsible for doing this to me?

I learned afterwards that Dr. Morris had contacted the social worker in charge of my case. But he had been unsuccessful in making anyone change their mind about me. As far as the social worker was concerned, the evidence showed my children were at great risk under my care. There was little anyone, even a doctor, could do about my reputation.

In the weeks that followed, I spent a lot of time in Dr.

Morris' office. I suspect he was worried that I would attempt suicide. Jerry was still in San Diego. Dr. Morris contacted him and asked if Jerry might come home early. As much as he wanted to, that was out of the question, Jerry said.

I was losing weight day by day. One afternoon in his office Dr. Morris broke the news: I was pregnant. I was going to have to do something about my weight loss given the upcoming delivery.

I was hysterical.

I don't want this baby, I screamed. I can't go through this anymore.

Dr. Morris took my hand.

Yes, you can, he said.

I did everything you told me, I said. Everything. It didn't help one little bit.

I know, Dr. Morris said. And I'm sorry. Sometimes the government does what it thinks it has to do. Sometimes, they're wrong. But you've got to try. You won't be going through this alone.

Dr. Morris arranged for me to see him at his office every day during the week. On weekends I was to meet him at the hospital.

When Jerry arrived home from San Diego, I could barely look him in the face.

Who's doing this to us, Jerry? I asked.

I don't know, sweetheart, he said. But I promise you I'll find out.

I asked him why he hadn't come home early when Dr. Morris asked him to.

I really needed you, Jerry, I said.

What would be the sense of that? he answered. I knew you were in good hands.

But, Jerry, this is happening to us.

Everything will be fine, he said. You'll see.

I didn't have the energy to continue. If Jerry felt I was badgering him, I knew I would get even less support than I was already.

Still, it bothers me, Jerry, I said.

Do you want a cup of tea? he asked.

Sure, I said.

Jerry went off to the kitchen. I could hear him filling the kettle with water and putting it on the stove.

I sank down into my chair. I didn't feel like getting up.

That night, after we went to bed, Jerry tried to be sweet to me. I turned and moved away from him. The pain inside my heart was too much. I felt like a stranger in my own bed, and in my own house.

I felt my mom didn't want to talk to me. I called her but she didn't say much. Neither did Myrna. What surprised me was how Jerry and Myrna got on. Jerry was now often on the phone with Myrna. This was a mystery to me. More than once the thought crossed my mind they were conspiring against me. I realized this was paranoid thinking on my part, and dismissed it. I mentioned to Anna how I felt

She said, You can't afford now to let your guard down.

I said I wouldn't.

Jerry agreed to see Dr. Morris with me. The following day Dr. Morris surprised me when he asked about my relationship with Jerry.

Have you ever thought of leaving your husband?

I was shocked.

I do believe in my marriage vows, I said. When I got married, I vowed this marriage would work no matter what.

Has Jerry ever hit you? Dr. Morris asked.

No, never, I said.

If he ever does, Dr. Morris said, I want you to promise

me you'll walk out. I'm here to help you any way I can.

Thank you, I said.

No need to thank me, he replied. I'm just happy to be here for you.

I turned eighteen that November. Two weeks after my birthday, Jerry brought home news that he had been assigned a shore station in Aldergrove, on the Lower Mainland. We would be moving to married quarters there. I was expecting the new baby in December. Jerry said he would take leave for a month so that we would have the time together for my delivery and our move.

We made arrangements with a moving company to pack our belongings and to ship them in mid-December to Aldergrove. The baby was born on December 15th. She was six and a half pounds, short and pudgy. She had beautiful blonde hair, and blue eyes. I named her Catherine Allison just because I liked the name.

Dr. Morris released us from the hospital on Christmas Eve. Jerry, Cathy and I went directly to the ferry to Vancouver. My mom had invited us to her place. I dreaded going there. I expected my mom and I would find it very hard to be together. But I was surprised. My mom took to Cathy right away. For reasons I couldn't understand (and still don't) she couldn't get enough of the baby.

Jerry and I moved into our new quarters in Aldergrove just before New Year's Eve. We moved into a yellow and white rancher on a treed cul-de-sac. There was a hobby farm next to us, with cows and horses and a few chickens. Jerry was given a forty-eight hour shift, eight hours on, eight hours off. Then he had four days off from work.

I liked our time living in Aldergrove. Life settled into a routine with Jerry doing his shifts and my taking care of the baby. The welfare office called me. A social worker came to the house three different occasions to visit and to see Cathy. I was on pins and needles each time. The worker said that as far as she could tell Jerry and I were perfect parents for Cathy. When I asked about Sarah, Colin and the baby returning to us, the worker said unfortunately that wouldn't be happening.

I was asked to an interview at the welfare office. This time Jerry came with me. I was surprised that the worker from Victoria was among the group of people there to meet with us. There were three or four other social workers. We were introduced to them all. The worker from Victoria said they were recommending that Jerry and I give up Colin, Sarah and Arlene for adoption. She said we would not be seeing them again in any case, whatever our decision was. We should permit them to be adopted. It would be in their best interest. This way we could be assured that they would be loved and cared for by their new families.

I had no argument remaining against what was being said. Everything I wanted to say I had said before. I have never felt hatred as I did that day. I hated what welfare was doing. Reluctantly, I signed the papers.

Jerry took us out for dinner that night. It was as though Jerry saw it as an occasion to celebrate. I couldn't understand why he wasn't feeling the same way I was. I felt as if my heart had been torn apart. I prayed our children had parents who loved them as much as I did. It didn't matter what anyone said about me. I would always love them.

Chapter Thirteen

One day Jerry came home with the news that we would be moving to Halifax. He had been assigned a two-year contract there in communications and then six weeks of further training at a Navy facility at Cornwallis, Nova Scotia. I was thrilled. I had never crossed the country before and thought it was a wonderful opportunity for us.

Cathy was a beautiful child, with long blonde hair and beautiful blue eyes. She was tall and willowy. In the interim, the bond between the two of us had grown very strong. The threat of welfare was over. And I was sure that Cathy would continue to be mine. No one on this earth could take her away from me. With that realization in place, my life started to level out. I could almost laugh again. And I was thrilled with other news I had gotten. My doctor had confirmed I was pregnant.

The movers were hired to pack up our belongings and ship them to Halifax. Armand and Carrie Radd, one of the first couples we had met in Aldergrove, were transferring to

Halifax at the same time. We agreed to meet when we got there.

During the beginning of this pregnancy I was sick. I couldn't keep anything down except for purple popsicles and water. The doctor said it was nerves and that unfortunately the move wasn't going to help. The pain I was feeling was enough to make me double over. Jerry said I was being stupid and that I was exaggerating the pain. He said I was feeling that way because of the move and the fact that we were driving a long way. I said that wasn't it. The pains came right in the middle of my rib cage and went straight through to my back. They were so severe I couldn't breathe. Since my doctor hadn't found anything else wrong, I kept the problem as much as possible to myself. Sometimes when the pain came, I would hide in the bathroom and throw up. After the pain calmed down a bit, I would wash my face and carry on with what I was doing.

While we were traveling, I was sick. Every time we stopped to eat I would throw up. Jerry got angry and said it was a waste of money to buy food for me when all I did was throw it up. We had made the back seat of the car into a playpen for Cathy. We made the back seat level with the front seats. That way, Cathy could watch out the front window while standing up and talk to us while we travelled. If she liked, she could sit down and play with her toys. And she could sleep when she felt like it. Because she was free and there were no restraints on what she did, she seemed to love traveling.

We stopped in Calgary to see my Uncle Ray and Aunty Gail. It was not something that Jerry had wanted to do but I had insisted. Jerry had a dislike for my aunt and uncle, and that dislike was returned in kind. I had no idea why. On my part, I was thrilled to see my aunt and uncle. It had been such a long time since I had seen them last. Cathy took to them right away. The three of them bonded almost immediately.

We stayed in Calgary for three days. I had several attacks of throwing up but I hid them from my aunt and uncle. Uncle Ray asked if I wanted to go to Three Hills to visit Grandma and Grandpa Blue Eyes.

Of course, I said.

Aunty Gail offered to babysit Cathy. Jerry decided he would visit the sights around town. It was April, cold and windy. As soon as we got to Three Hill's cemetery, the wind stopped and it was almost warm. I had brought roses and I put these on the graves.

Uncle Ray said he knew I'd had a lot of trouble in my short life and that he was going to find out what was going on. He asked me to promise that, if I needed him, I would call. He said he didn't care what time of day or night it was.

I promised that I would. Then one of my pains came and I doubled over. When he saw the extent of the pain, Uncle Ray wanted to rush me to the hospital. I said I couldn't do that. Jerry would be furious. It would pass. My own doctor had said it was nerves—nothing more. Uncle Ray said he was of the mind that there was something seriously wrong with me.

You're white as a sheet, he said.

I assured him I'd be fine. Uncle Ray took me in his arms and rocked me like a baby. Little by little, I felt better.

Aunty Gail had a big dinner ready for us when we got back.

Jerry, Cathy and I left the next day. I hated saying goodbye to my aunt and uncle. Uncle Ray took me aside and told me he loved me. He said he had wished I could have been his daughter. That way, I would not have gone through what I had. I had never spoken to my aunt and uncle about losing my three children. I assumed they did know but that they had decided not to bring the matter up with me.

When Jerry and I arrived in Winnipeg, there was two feet of snow on the ground. It was very cold. Jerry's mom lived on a farm outside the city. The log farm-house had no running water or indoor toilet and was heated by a wood stove in the kitchen. At night Cathy slept in the bed with us so that she would be warm. There was a heavy quilt on the bed but the wind and cold came through the chinks in the logs of the house. I had never been that cold before. Being from the west coast, I had never seen so much snow and decided I never wanted to see that much snow again as long as I lived. I was still sick. Every time I didn't feel well, the only choice I had was to run outside and cross the field to the outhouse. The smell, once I was inside, didn't make it any better.

The visit was very hard for me. I felt that Jerry's mom didn't like me and put up with me only on Jerry's account. After a week at the farm Jerry said he wanted us to stay another week. It was a morning that I had been exceptionally sick. I gave Jerry a damning look and told him straight out that if he didn't get me to some place that had running water and an indoor bathroom, I would start walking. I was surprised when he agreed that we should leave.

We drove through the snow all the next day. We were driving an older car and it was a good car for the snow. We made good time. It took us six days to reach Nova Scotia. Jerry yelled at me a good part of the time for being sick and not being able to keep anything down. The pain I was feeling was so intense that I had to lie down. I couldn't look after Cathy and Jerry had to watch her and drive at the same time. I spent most of the time curled up in the front seat of the car. I lived on popsicles during the whole trip.

We arrived in Digby on a Monday morning. We found a room at a place called The Teacup Inn. When the owner saw me, she said she was worried about me. She said there was a doctor uptown whom she could recommend.

Jerry took me to the doctor's office. The doctor weighed me and said I had lost twenty-five pounds in the couple weeks since we had left Vancouver. His diagnosis was that I had gallstones. He said being pregnant didn't help matters. Because of the pregnancy, I couldn't take any drugs to remedy the gallstones. But the doctor gave me vitamins. He had me enter the hospital in Digby and stay overnight to be treated for dehydration. I could barely walk.

It was a very small hospital. The nurses and doctors were so kind to me. As soon as I was assigned a bed, the nurse on duty swaddled me up tightly in a warm blanket. It felt wonderful. I snuggled down and went into a deep sleep. The next morning I was released, and I was able to be back with Cathy and Jerry.

During the time we lived there, I got to like Digby, Nova Scotia. It was a quaint little place, especially on Saturdays. It surprised me that you couldn't buy a drop of liquor after twelve noon. You would see everyone heading to the liquor store in the morning. Some people bought as much as they could carry. And they would sell it on the weekend for a tidy profit.

I believe the tide at Digby is the highest in the world. When the tide was up, it was way up. And when the tide was out, the boats in the harbour were almost resting on the sand. I thought it funny how the fishermen didn't need boats to fish: when the tide was out, they strung huge nets above the sand. These looked like so many volleyball nets. When the tide came in, the fish were caught in the netting. When the tide went back out, the fishermen went out on the sand and retrieved their catch. I understood in this way they made a very good living.

Jerry, Cathy, and I walked down to the docks one day and bought a live lobster. We brought it home to our room and filled the bathtub and put the lobster in. I named the lobster George. When the time came for George to be cooked, I couldn't do it. Instead, I went out for a walk. I couldn't eat dinner later. Jerry had no problem doing so. He said George was very tasty.

I found that I loved Digby. The first time we were out for a drive, we saw two oxen pulling a cart and its driver. The oxen where white and had long, curled horns. I had never seen real oxen before.

The age you could legally marry in Nova Scotia at that time was thirteen years of age. The government was submitting a bill in the legislature to raise the age of consent to sixteen. It was voted down. I got to know one of our neighbors who had married that early. She was twenty-nine—and a grandmother.

I made so many good friends in Digby. Many of them were poor. Some of them had very little furniture. They had apple boxes for tables and chairs. They grew their own food and put up preserves for the winter months. Sometimes their clothes were old and thread-bare. Despite their poverty, I found great love among them. They were wonderful teachers to me.

It came time for us to go to Halifax for the rest of Jerry's assignment. The weekend before we were to leave, my friends threw a farewell party for me. I received some mementoes from my friends that I have kept to this day: a pair of lobster salt and pepper shakers, and a seashell.

It was a sad day when we left Digby. I felt for the first time in my life that I had been accepted for who I was. I felt I had not been judged by any of our friends whom I'd gotten to know. I wondered how it was that welfare was leaving us alone, and I thanked the universe for the reprieve.

I was still losing weight, and had lost thirty-three pounds in all. The doctor was worried about me. He said he couldn't do surgery on the gallstones until the baby was born. He said that they might have to take the baby very early if the pains continued and were out of control.

Jerry made a trip to Halifax and rented an apartment for us. Our friends, Armand and Carrie, were already in the area and living in a place outside of town. Of course, they invited us to visit and we accepted the invitation. Armand and Carrie had a small house right on the shore of the cove. It was beautiful to sit outside and watch the water and see the boats going by. Carrie was shocked to see me and how much weight I had lost. She offered to take care of Cathy when I went into hospital to have the baby.

When the time for my delivery got closer, we took Carrie up on her offer. I was scared but I had no choice in the matter. Jerry had to work and had no vacation time left. The weekend before the baby was due, we took Cathy to Armand and Carrie's. All my fears from before came rushing back. I was scared I would never see Cathy again.

When my time for the baby came, Jerry rushed me to the hospital. Three days later, I gave to birth to a beautiful girl. We named her Shelley Marie. I liked the name and it seemed to suit her. Shelley was a big baby, twenty-three inches tall and eight pounds nine ounces. I was in the hospital for about ten days, still sick from my gallstones. The doctor said I had to stabilize before I could return home. Finally, he allowed me to take Shelley home.

I was scheduled again for the hospital to have my gallstones removed. I kept in touch with my doctor because he was afraid I might have jaundice or liver failure. Carrie offered to babysit both children when I went into hospital. I accepted her offer and prayed that the girls would be okay without me.

One afternoon, a week before my appointment at the hospital, I started having pains. By the time Jerry came home, I was trying hard not to scream with the pain. Jerry immediately called the doctor. The doctor asked if my skin was off-colour. Jerry said it was. The doctor said to get me to the hospital right away.

When I arrived at the hospital, the doctor took one look at me and said I'd be having surgery in the morning. I cried. I was scared. A nurse brought in a mirror to show me that my skin was yellow. My eyes were yellow, too.

If something isn't done soon, there's a chance you could die, the doctor said. You wouldn't want that to happen—not with two beautiful little girls.

Afterwards, I cried. I settled down and the drugs took hold and I slept.

The next morning arrived. I was still feeling afraid. My skin and eyes were even more yellow then the night before. The doctor came to see me before the surgery. He said I would be just fine and that when I woke up, I would be sore. He promised that the stones would be gone. And then I would just have to get better.

When I came out of the surgery, I was sick. My recovery was slow. Jerry and Carrie brought the children up to see me a few times. I was still weak but after two weeks the doctor said I could go home. The doctor gave me my forty-six stones, some the size of gravel, and some larger. He said it was a wonder I was still here in this world.

The day I went home was a wonderful one for me. Jerry brought the children back from Carrie's house and we were all together again.

Jerry helped me at night when he got home from work. By the time he came home at night, I was so tired I could not make his supper. Very often, I just sat down with the girls and let him take over. My strength came back faster than the doctor wanted it to. He said I should rest more.

Oh, sure, I said.

He laughed and said for me to take it easy as much as possible.

This was one of the happiest times in my married life. Jerry was away at work for long hours. And I had time to spend with Shelley and Cathy. We fell into a routine: Jerry heading off to work in the morning, and I with the whole day in front of me and nothing else much to do but decide how the girls and I might spend the day.

Jerry's birthday was Election Day in Halifax. The weather forecast was for sun with a chance of showers. That day we had sun, rain, a foot of snow, ice, thunder, and lightning—all in one day. There was not a car moving. If I remember correctly, the turnout at the polls that year was very poor.

Chapter Fourteen

Our friend, Armand, had been sent back to Victoria as he had been accepted for officer training. It was time for us to say goodbye to him and Carrie. I knew I would miss them. Armand and Carrie had been true friends.

Whenever we had visited them at their house, the girls had made Armand and Carrie's their second home. Armand called Cathy his puppy dog because she was the first one to greet him when he came home from work. Lots of evenings you could see Armand walking along the shore at their home with Cathy in his arms, the two of them having a heart-to-heart talk, as much as a two-and-a-half-year-old can have with an adult.

Often, when I saw Armand and Cathy together, I wished that Jerry would be the same with his girls. But to no avail. Most of the time, Jerry was standoffish. He did what he had to do. I can't say Jerry ignored the girls. But there was not the bond between the girls and Jerry that I wished for.

Our time to return to the west coast came. Jerry had been

transferred to a ship out of Victoria for the next two years. Before leaving, I went to the doctor for my last check up. I was told I was pregnant. I cried at the news. I was frightened. I was going back to Victoria where so many bad things had happened before.

The movers came to pack up the apartment. It was difficult to decide what to keep for our trip and what not to. We decided we were going to take our time driving back and do some sightseeing along the way. We still had the same car we had driven to Halifax. Just as we had done on our first trip, we made a play pen in the back seat for the girls. They could play when they wanted to, and sleep when they were tired.

Cathy was the sweetest little girl, and fully trained. Although she was under a year, Shelley had trained herself, and had thrown her baby bottle away. That was Shelley— so independent. She wanted to do everything herself. She barely let anyone else do anything for her. Shelley was as tall as Cathy. If one hadn't known better, one would have taken the girls to be twins.

Cathy was the quieter of the two, very much a lady and very sedate. Shelley, on the other hand, was adventurous and full of inquisitiveness. She needed to know the answer to everything and how things were done.

We stopped at Niagara Falls. We booked ourselves into a motel and took the girls to view the sights. The falls were spectacular. Because the girls were so young, we couldn't take the tourist boat ride but watched the falls from a distance. At that time, I didn't understand the magic of water. I could have stayed for hours and just watched the falls, listening to the sound of the cascading water and feeling the power of it. Each second, as you watched, you saw something different. One minute you would see a brilliant rainbow and the next moment the rainbow would be gone. I could see the water drops dancing. I could see water sprites forming and rising from the spray and joining hands together.

We stopped near Winnipeg to visit Jerry's mom. She was living in a small town a hundred miles south of the city. I met Jerry's brother, Tom, for the very first time. Tom was much older than Jerry—two decades older—and had long since retired. I put on my bravest face and crossed my fingers that everything would be fine.

Because Jerry's mom had a small house, Jerry and I and the girls stayed at the local resort lodge. The resort was nothing to compare to the mountains I knew from home. These hills were not very high at all. But I smiled and kept my opinions to myself and made complimentary comments about the hills and the resort and the little cabins that they rented out to tourists.

The town was very small. There were no more than two hundred people living there at the time. The town was in the valley, and it was very pretty. To cool themselves from the summer heat, the girls went wading in a creek that ran by. Occasionally, we would see wild turkeys come out from the underbrush.

It happened that one of Jerry's relatives was getting married and we were invited to the wedding. The girls were invited, too. On the night of the wedding, I dressed the girls in their best dresses. Both of them, being so independent, were very much little ladies. I was so proud of them. They were the hit of the wedding. Neither one of them wanted to go home to bed. I did my best to be polite. I wanted everyone to have a good opinion of me. In the end, I felt that most of them liked me for who I was. I felt they had taken the time to get to know me. Jerry's mom, however, still didn't like me. And she didn't seem to care for the girls.

The time came for us to leave. We decided we would visit my Uncle Ray in Calgary. I was so happy to see Uncle Ray and Aunt Gail again. The girls took to them right away. We went to see the sights in Calgary while Jerry took our car and went away on his own.

Uncle Ray and Aunty Gail took us all out to Three Hills, where my grandma and grandpa had lived. Their house was still standing but it was old and uncared for—so different from the way I remembered it. We went to the cemetery where my grandma and grandpa and my Uncle Pete were buried. I took flowers for the grave sites. I took the girls aside and tried to explain who these people had been and how much they had meant to me. But, of course, the girls were much too young to comprehend.

My aunt took the girls and myself everywhere. She took us shopping and helped dress the girls and bought them toys. After the girls went to bed, my aunt and uncle and I would play cards and laugh and enjoy each other's company. When Jerry would come in, I would ask him where he had been. He would just say he had been around.

One evening Jerry came in and told me to pack. He said we would be leaving as soon as the girls got up in the morning. I looked at Aunt Gail and Uncle Ray and shrugged. It seemed our visit was over. As we left, I kept thinking of how much fun the girls and I had had and how much I owed my aunt and uncle for making us feel so much at home. I knew that my aunt and uncle still did not like Jerry. I did not understand why they felt that way.

We drove to Banff and then through the national park. At one point along the way, Jerry pulled over for us to take a look at a moose grazing at the side of the road. Jerry stopped the car and I rolled the window down a bit. The moose came over to the window and stuck his nose in. I scratched it. He snorted and walked off into the forest. What a thrill it was to touch a wild animal!

We drove to Vancouver, stopping only for gas and rest rooms, with Jerry and I taking turns driving. We arrived at my mom's house. My mom fell in love with the girls, especially Shelley. Shelley, in turn, seemed to form a strong bond with her. It surprised me to see my mom talking and laughing with Shelley. I could not have predicted nor imagined it. It was a mystery to me how my mom was able to attend to Shelley in ways she had never thought to do with me.

The time came for us to go to Vancouver Island and to find a place to live. We found a motel in Victoria and stayed there for a week. In the meantime, we were able to find a house to buy. It was almost brand new, had three bedrooms, and a yard. We paid twelve thousand dollars and were able to move in as soon as the papers were signed. As soon as we got settled, we contacted our friends, Armand and Carrie, and got together with them. Uncle Armand and Cathy took up where they had left off in Halifax. The two of them were inseparable. Armand's nickname for Cathy was "George" and she loved it.

One day Jerry arrived home from work with a dog in his arms. It was a male basset hound. The dog's name was Sam. He was a tricolour: black, white and brown, and apparently two years old. I thought he looked about ten. His previous owner had been a well-known writer and journalist. Supposedly, Sam had been hit by a truck and his former owner had spent two thousand dollars on restoring him to health.

The girls were thrilled with Sam. They set right away to teaching Sam to bark since he had never learned to do so. What antics there were to get Sam to make that first sound. And when he did give his first bark, we all converged on him, praising and hugging him. Oh, that dog was loved.

There were times when my old fears would return to me and I would lie awake afraid that I might lose the girls. I would tell myself there was no reason for me to feel this way any longer. The girls were well-adjusted and I found raising them such a joy. As I anticipated the upcoming birth of the next baby, my fears rose up once again stronger than ever.

Joseph John was premature by three weeks and weighed five pounds. His weight dropped immediately to four pounds. He was placed in an incubator for a week while we waited for him to stabilize. There were cards and presents from friends, but nothing from Jerry to mark the occasion. All my previous feelings of inadequacy returned. I was afraid to touch the baby, afraid I might do something wrong, afraid that I might lose him.

Joseph was so tiny, his face small and wrinkled. His skin was yellow from jaundice and red from being born. But he responded quickly to being taken care of, and in a very short time was gaining weight and enjoying the attention of the girls.

Chapter Fifteen

Jerry was still suffering from arthritis and was given a medical discharge. We sold our house and moved to Richmond. Jerry got a job with a credit agency doing credit reporting and seemed to like the work.

One weekend, while Jerry and I were out for a drive in the suburbs with the kids, we saw a kennel for sale. Jerry and I were immediately interested. The girls said yes. We put an offer on the kennel and it was accepted. We were in the basset hound raising business—or at least I was. The house and kennel itself were older buildings but not in bad repair. They required some needed maintenance and paint. The kennel was on five acres and a creek ran through the property. When you walked behind the kennels and house into the forest, you had a wonderful place to sit and think by yourself or to have a picnic. The children and I and Sammy spent many hours out back.

Time has a way of slipping by unnoticed. Days come and days go and before you know it another year or two has passed by without too much difficulty. My days were filled with preparing the kids for school, with bake sales, and parent-teacher conferences. Jerry never went to one parent-teacher conference. He said he was always too busy or had some other place to go. I took the girls to brownies, guides, and to sports. Every time I tried to involve Jerry in any of the children's activities, it was always indifference on his part. His usual comment was: you do it, I'm not interested.

Living with Jerry was like living with a brother or a distant relative. Our love life had dwindled to nothing. There were no shared feelings of caring. I still thought I loved him. With our problems with welfare far behind us, I thought our life would get better. I knew that Jerry really missed the service. In the Navy he had been a free man, able to come and go and do as he pleased. He would leave and he would be gone for three or four months. When he returned, I had always been glad to see him and tried to pick up where we had left off. Without the service in our lives, that part changed. There was no leaving and returning. No fond farewells, no romantic homecomings.

Sometimes I wondered why Jerry had stayed with me all this time without once talking of leaving. I thought he really must love me. And, of course, I asked myself the same question: why did I continue to live with him? I knew part of the answer. I was too afraid to leave. After all I'd been through, I wasn't about to risk losing my family for a second time. I thought to myself, It's like a piece of string. You hang onto that string. It isn't much. You know you could have so much more. But you hang onto the string. It's not much— but it's better than nothing.

Joseph had just started school. We were doing a lot of painting and Joseph had a wonderful time with a paint brush in his hands even though he got more paint on him than on what he was painting. This was a wonderful time for us. Cathy and I were very close. Shelley had her own agenda. She was very much a leader. She listened to me—but just barely. She loved her dad, and listened more to him than to me. Joseph and I had a very strong bond and we would spend hours together talking or reading together or walking Sammy.

One day, I accompanied a friend, Alice, to a dog show. I watched the basset hounds since I wanted to see other dogs like Sammy. After the winners of that group were announced, I went over to talk to their owners. Their names were Pat and John Bishop. They had been raising basset hounds for years. We struck it off right away. John worked in construction. He and Pat had three children of their own. They asked if I would like to bring Jerry and the kids to their home for dinner that Saturday night. I accepted the invitation and said I would confirm once I talked to Jerry.

When I told Jerry of the invitation, he was upset. He said I should not have made plans without talking with him first. He did agree reluctantly to go.

When we arrived at Pat and John's house, John was on the roof replacing some of the roof tiles. He came down and I introduced Jerry. John said that unfortunately he had to finish his repairs. Jerry offered to help. John accepted and they went to work.

Cathy, Shelley and Joseph went off to play with Pat's children. That left Pat and I to ourselves. Pat showed me the kennel and their ten dogs.

This invitation led to further conversations. Jerry said he liked the idea of operating a boarding kennel but that we were not going to breed or show dogs. I had other ideas about that. I argued that the money we made boarding dogs would cover the costs of raising and showing them.

The children loved the idea of more bassets. Sammy was still the apple of our eye. He was so spoiled. His favorite activity on a Saturday or Sunday morning was to get into bed with one of the children, usually Cathy. He would put his head on her pillow and she would cover him with her blanket. She would put Sammy's droopy ears over his eyes to shut out the light. Every time Cathy went through this ritual, Sammy would fall asleep and snore, just like a human. Sometimes, when I went into Cathy's room, I laughed at the sight: Cathy and Sam sound asleep in bed, Cathy's arms around Sam, and Sam snoring loudly, his ears draped over his eyes.

Our next dog was a tricoloured female, Baby Doll, as we liked to call her. We bought her as a puppy. Baby's ears were so long that she regularly tripped over them. When it was time to feed her, we pinned her ears back so that they wouldn't fall into her dish.

Our days were not to continue in this way. One spring morning we received another brutal blow. In the early hours of the morning, Jerry and I woke suddenly to the smell of smoke and anguished screams. I recognized right away that it was seven-year-old Shelley.

Rushing into Shelley's room, I wasn't prepared for what I saw. Shelley's body was in flames. A crackling fire shot upward from her. She was screaming. Jerry threw a blanket over her and rolled her onto the floor.

I ran upstairs to see if Joseph and Cathy were in any danger. It was clear that the fire was limited to Shelley's room. Joseph and Cathy had woken to the screaming as Jerry and I had been.

I ran back to Shelley's room. She was screaming. I told Jerry that I was calling the ambulance.

No, said Jerry, you're going to drive her to the hospital.

I can't, I said.

You will too, he said.

Jerry picked up Shelley and laid her down in the back seat of the car. I got in and started the car. I was so frightened I could hardly put the car in gear.

Shelley continued to scream. There were very few cars on the road. At one point, there was a car behind me. By my driving, the driver could tell that something was wrong. He signaled for me to pull over. When he saw the situation, he motioned that he would drive. I slid over to the passenger seat and he took the wheel. He drove the car down the highway at break-neck speed.

When we arrived at the hospital, the man jumped out of the car and ran in. In a matter of moments, a doctor and a number of nurses were taking Shelley out of the car and putting her onto a gurney.

Please don't let her die, I kept saying. Please.

Inside the admitting room, I lost consciousness.

When I came to, a nurse was by my side. She said I was in shock. She gave me a sedative. After a little time had passed, I was allowed to call home. Cathy and Joseph were fine and were staying home from school. Sylvia, who rented a basement suite from us, was staying with them.

Jerry had gone to work. He had called to say he had arrived there. He had been ten minutes late. I could not believe that Jerry had abandoned us. Didn't his daughter's life matter more? How could Jerry have made such a decision?

I thought, If Shelley dies because of his ignorance, I will take the other children and I will be long gone. Please don't let Shelley die, please.

I waited that day and all that evening. The doctors said they did not know if Shelley would survive. She had been placed on the critical list. She had sustained second degree burns to thirty per cent of her body. I was not allowed by her side. Shelley had been placed in isolation for fear of her contracting an infection. I could watch her from the other side of a glass but couldn't go near her.

Jerry showed up at the hospital at seven in the evening. I couldn't talk to him, even less look at him. The doctor asked Jerry why he hadn't called the emergency number. Jerry said he had thought the best decision was to take Shelley to the hospital immediately. The doctor told him he'd been wrong, that calling emergency would have gotten Shelley faster medical attention.

Jerry replied very defiantly that it was none of the doctor's business what he did—or what he would do in the future.

The doctor asked me to go home. There was nothing we could do to help. The hospital would call us immediately if there was any change in Shelley's condition.

The days that followed I went to the hospital every day but was still not allowed in to see Shelley. Very seldom did Jerry go to the hospital. When the day came for me to see Shelley, the attending nurse told me to be prepared for the worst. I should not let Shelley see me crying.

I was given a surgical gown, and cap, and boots to cover my shoes. A nurse accompanied me into the room. She held my hand. I was allowed five minutes with Shelley—no more.

Shelley had been badly burned, from her chin to her knees. Her fingers were joined together by the fire's heat. Her neck was joined to one shoulder. Somehow, her face had escaped the fire's wrath.

Shelley, Mom is here, I said. I'm here. If you need me, I'm here.

Shelley was so sedated it was hard to know if she heard me. I told Shelley that I loved her and that she was very special to me and that she was going to get better. The nurse told me it was time to go.

Shelley, I love you, I said. Don't you forget—I love you. I'll be right outside.

I went out. There, I broke down and cried.

Is she going to make it? I asked the nurse. Please, tell me she is.

The nurse said it was too early to tell.

Come back tomorrow, she said.

When I arrived home, Jerry was already there. I told him he was going with me to the hospital the next day and that he had to see his daughter. He told me he didn't want to. I said I didn't care. He was Shelley's father and he had a responsibility to see her.

I said, Never mind responsibility. It's called love. And if you don't or can't love her enough to put your ego aside, what kind of man are you?

I didn't wait for him to reply. I turned and walked out of the room.

Cathy and Joseph both wanted to visit Shelley. I said they couldn't and that Shelley was not well enough for them to see her.

The next day Jerry and I went to the hospital together. We went through the same procedure as I had the day before. Both of us were clothed in cap and gown in order to see Shelley. Jerry showed no emotion. The nurse held my hand. I kept telling Shelley over and over that she was going to be fine and she would be coming home. Jerry never spoke a word. Before the five minutes were up, Jerry had already left the room.

When I came out, I was in tears. I asked Jerry why he hadn't talked to Shelley. He said that Shelley wouldn't have heard him anyway. He said he guessed that Shelley was not going to make it.

I was furious.

How can you possibly say that about your child? I told him. You bastard. She is going to make it.

Jerry and I pieced together afterward how the fire had started. We wondered how Shelley happened to have matches. Neither Jerry nor I smoked. The matches we did keep for emergencies were kept high up in a cupboard.

Joseph and Cathy said that Shelley had found the matches outside. Someone must have dropped them. The rest was fairly clear. Shelley had struck a match and dropped it. Her pajamas had been more than enough fuel. The material had instantly ignited

In six months, Shelley came home. The doctors advised us not to give Shelley special attention. We were told to treat her like any other child. As much as I felt otherwise, I tried to be hopeful and encouraging. It was good to have Shelley home.

When Shelley was able to return to school, some of the other children were cruel to her, calling her terrible names. I visited the school principal to see what could be done. The principal said he would try to help. As a result, conditions did improve at school, but Shelley continued to be depressed. She no longer had the same interest in things that she'd had before the fire.

One evening, while Jerry and I were outside with Sammy, a neighbor came by. He said he knew that Shelley had been burned and was having a difficult time. He asked if a service club he belonged to might become involved with Shelley. Jerry and I both said we would be grateful for any help Shelley might get.

Within a very few days we had a telephone call from the club. Two members of the club made an appointment to meet Shelley and ourselves. They mentioned the work that was being done on burned children at a hospital in Texas. They described some of the surgical procedures they thought could help Shelley's physical condition.

We asked how much it would cost us to send Shelley to the hospital for treatment. We were told the treatment would be free. This offer was in keeping with the club's creed: to help children in need. Jerry and I talked it over, then discussed it with Shelley. She said she would go. Within two weeks Shelley was on her way to the hospital.

Shelley had six weeks of treatment. She underwent a couple different surgeries and skin grafts. When it came time for her to return, Joseph, Cathy and I went to the airport to welcome her home. When we saw her, we all broke into tears.

Shelley walked towards us with her head held high. Her fingers were no different from our own. The girl walking towards us looked like any other eight-year-old girl you might meet.

Two members of the club came to visit Shelley within a few days of her return. They reported that the doctors in the hospital had been extremely happy with the results of Shelley's surgery. However, Shelley would have to be admitted to Children's Hospital in Oregon for follow-up visits. Of course, Jerry and I agreed that she would continue with the treatments.

We were given complimentary tickets to the circus which happened to be coming to town in ten days. Who doesn't love the circus? The morning of the event, I got a telephone call from a club member. He asked if Shelley would be willing to walk out to center stage that evening and present flowers to a member of the provincial legislature. Shelley said she would be happy to.

That night we were accompanied to a special VIP box. I had bought Shelley a new jumper that was a beautiful shade of orange, and a white blouse to wear under it. With black patent shoes and white socks and her jumper, Shelley looked beautiful.

At half-time Shelley was accompanied to centre stage and introduced to the audience. She was given a bouquet of roses to present to Charlotte Whitby, the member of the provincial legislature. The announcer told of Shelley's injuries and her treatment in Texas.

As Shelley crossed the stage, the members of the audience applauded. They chanted, Go Shelley Go. There was a standing ovation as she presented the bouquet of roses to the woman who stood at centre stage. Charlotte Whitby hugged Shelley. They stood and talked for the few minutes they had left.

During the next week Shelley got quite a bit of fan mail. From that time on, Shelley found being at school easier but she was often moody and angry. No doubt she felt angry about how much her life had changed as a consequence of the fire. Shelley had always been strong-willed but after the fire she stubbornly refused anything asked of her. At these times, Pat and John proved to be good friends. They often took Shelley for a few hours at a time when I found myself unsympathetic to her moods. There were days her moods were so bad, I didn't know where to turn or what to do.

Meanwhile, Jerry and I had started our own financial consulting company. We had a few good clients and I was working very hard to make it successful. The best part of my life was still my children, and our dogs.

Chapter Sixteen

One day I got the idea that Cathy and Shelley might like skating lessons. Both girls said they were interested.

The first day on the ice, Cathy was stiff as a board and afraid to move. Shelley, on the other hand, took one step onto the ice and off she went. It soon became evident that Shelley was a natural on the ice. Within two weeks Shelley had mastered skills that took normally six months to acquire. Within a few months, Shelley was already doing solo performances at the annual skating show.

Cathy, on the other hand, proved to be an artist. I wanted her to take art lessons but she said she didn't want to. She preferred to paint on her own. For Cathy's birthday I purchased her a piano. I thought that if I could support Shelley's skating, I could as easily support Cathy in her interests.

Of all my children, I spent the most time with Cathy. Often I wondered how my other children were. Were they well and happy? Sometimes I wanted to tell my children about their older sisters and brother. But I didn't have the courage. I was afraid they would blame me for the loss of the other children. I was afraid they would not believe the story I so much wanted to tell them. I felt it was a secret I might have to keep forever.

One day, after my menstrual period had started, I became alarmed by the amount of blood I was losing. By the second day I realized I was hemorrhaging. I got myself to the hospital right away. When I arrived at emergency, I did not have to wait long before I was seen. I was taken in and wrapped in a warm blanket and examined by a doctor. He said I was not to leave the hospital until I underwent a hysterectomy. My life was in danger. His opinion was that I would likely not survive another period like this one.

I was put on intravenous and not allowed to move. Jerry arrived at the hospital that evening. A friend of mine had called him earlier in the day. Jerry was apologetic but gave no excuse for being as late as he was. I said very little. I was past caring.

Within two days I underwent surgery. The doctor assured me it was the best decision given the danger I faced. Five days later, I was out of hospital. I needed to get back to work, I reasoned. I had a clean bill of health and no longer had any reason to stay.

Shortly after this time in my life, I happened to meet the mayor of Surrey. I had approached the municipality of Surrey because there was no legal provision for the operation of a hobby kennel within its boundaries.

I made an appointment to meet the mayor, Larry Bleecker, to propose a bylaw which would define a kennel and its operation. Larry and I started chatting. Eventually, we put our heads together and wrote up a bylaw that, if I am correct, stands to this day.

Our friendship did not stop with the writing of the bylaw. I was invited to meet Larry's wife, and joined the two of them for coffee and conversation on several occasions. The more I got to know Larry, the more I respected him. I started going to Surrey council meetings on a fairly regular basis. During break, often the members of council and Larry would chat with those of us who attended.

As time passed, Larry asked if I would be interested in joining his political party. Larry had put his name forward as leader of the party. I said I would be delighted to do so.. I felt Larry was a good candidate and wanted to support his election. I asked Jerry if he would join. He agreed.

The two of us worked hard on Larry's campaign. There was much to do. Telephones were set up for volunteers, like ourselves, to use. We called voters to solicit their support for the party. There were barbecues and cocktail parties to arrange. Constituents were invited to these and from among them volunteers were brought on board. My job was to make sure these arrangements happened smoothly.

The leadership convention was held at a nearby ski resort. I attended as a delegate for Larry. Jerry attended as an alternate delegate. I had never been to a convention before and was surprised by the marching and shouting and screaming. A friend of mine was supporting Charlotte Whitby as leader. He shouted her name out to me in the middle of the convention floor and I shouted back just as loudly Larry's name. We marched together arm in arm. Not surprisingly, before the weekend was over, my voice was gone.

One of the candidates by the name of Ken Sweeney crossed the convention floor in support of our candidate, pronouncing, "This candidate is for you". This was the swing vote that Larry needed to win. The response to the announcement of the victory was tremendous. The entire convention center exploded with cheering and shouting and clapping. There was such a spontaneous outpouring of emotion that my head swam. Never before had I experienced such a powerful charge of feeling. It was exhilarating.

One day at the resort I managed to get away by myself. I took a walk part way up the ski hill. I found a place to sit and thought about my life and reflected on the past. I wondered what would come my way next. The fragrance of the meadow flowers was carried to me by the breeze. The trees moved gently above me. I felt totally at ease. I looked up at the bright blue sky and the white clouds and was touched by the wonder and beauty of them. I realized that, as difficult as my life had been, I had survived. I had been able to handle what had been given to me. I felt secure in the thought that I would be able to handle whatever the future brought.

Jim, an acquaintance I had made through the political party, happened to be walking by. I invited him to join me. We ended up talking for a half hour. Jim owned a restaurant on the North Shore. He mentioned he was having difficulty with his business. He said it was not doing as well as he had hoped.

I made some suggestions as to what I thought might help. Jim was very appreciative. He offered to buy me lunch. We headed down the hill and agreed on a restaurant. There we found Larry, and his wife, and their close friends. Jerry, as well, had joined them for lunch. Jim and I were invited to join the celebration.

The provincial election soon followed the leadership convention. Both Jerry and I were invited to help Larry further in his campaign. I was scared out of my mind. I had never been involved in politics. At my first cocktail party I stood in a corner, unsure of myself, thinking everyone else was so much more intelligent than I. At one point in the evening, Roger Stinton, an incumbent MLA came over to me and introduced himself. Charlotte Whitby joined us. Roger put me immediately at ease. He said my work on gaining Larry the party leadership had come to his attention. He asked whether I would help him on his campaign.

I had put my heart and soul into helping Larry win the leadership. I appreciated that my contribution had been recognized. I told Roger my loyalty was to Larry and to helping him get elected Premier. Roger took my hand. He introduced me, first to one person, then to another. By the end of the evening I had met everyone.

Charlotte came up to me very quietly and took me aside. She asked if, by any chance, my daughter, Shelley, had been the young girl who had presented flowers to her at the circus. I said that Shelley had been very pleased to have had the honor. Charlotte's gaze softened. She gave me a hug and asked me to tell her all about Shelley and how she was doing. I said that Shelley was doing well and progressing rapidly at figure skating. I said that Shelley was learning so quickly that we had arranged a professional teacher for her. Charlotte said that she knew someone who could help in Shelley's training. She said she would be in touch soon.

Quite quickly, the connection between Charlotte and Shelley became a topic of discussion among everyone at the party. Larry took me aside and gave me his business card. On the back of the card he wrote his cell number. He said it was his private telephone number and would appreciate me not sharing it with anyone else. He said if I ever needed his help, I was to call him.

The election was quickly upon us. I was thrown into the inner circle of the party. Between working at our own business and working for Larry, I did not have time for much else. The day of the election Jerry and I started work at five in the morning, meeting the other volunteers at election headquarters. We worked hard all day. I oversaw the volunteers whose job it was to contact party supporters. The volunteers arranged rides to the polls for those who needed them. By early afternoon, I had not had time for a coffee break. I was asked if I would serve as a scrutineer at one of the polling booths. I said I would. I picked up my credentials on the way. As the polls closed, I helped oversee the counting of the ballots. We took the locked ballot box into a back room and under the eye of the deputy, we started the count. Our political party was far ahead. And, so it was elsewhere. The party had won with a clear majority. Larry was Premier.

Several days later I received a telephone call from Larry. He invited me to Victoria where he was to be sworn in as Premier. Larry said that he wanted those of us who had worked so hard on his behalf to be able to attend the ceremony.

I asked Jerry if he would like to go—but already knew the answer. Jerry said he had other things to do. I could go, if I liked. But I would have to go alone.

Two weeks later, Charlotte telephoned me and invited me to join her on the trip to the island. I said I would love to. We boarded one of the buses leased for the occasion. There were many others there who had worked in support of the party. Everyone was in a celebratory mood. There was lots of laughing and talking.

I had a minute for my own private thoughts. I thought how lucky I was to be there. I felt so accepted. I thought about Sarah, Colin and Arlene. Where might they be living? They would be teenagers by now. How were they doing?

My thoughts were soon interrupted by Charlotte and Roger. They informed me I had been invited to join the Premier-elect, his family, and his friends at the podium. I was thrilled to be included.

It was a bright warm day on our arrival in the capital city. There was no need for a coat. A business jacket was fine. I was so nervous being part of the ceremony. Larry and his wife welcomed us as we arrived. I was shown where I was to stand at the podium. I was enthralled by the building, by its aged patina and stately elegance. There were beautiful flowers and wonderful statues and brilliant, shining wood polished to its brightest.

The ceremony took place at eleven in the morning. The pipers played, as well as the Navy band. Hearing the Navy band brought back memories of my life as a young mother and wife. I stood with tears in my eyes, enthralled by the proceedings. For me, there was an added sweetness to the ceremony. For the very first time in my life, I was receiving recognition for my efforts.

Perhaps, all along I had been mistaken. Perhaps, I was worthy, after all.

Charlotte was as good as her word. A month after Larry's swearing-in, I got a telephone call from a professional figure skater who taught out of North Vancouver. Ron said he had been asked by Charlotte to contact me.

We talked at some length about Shelley and her skating ability. Ron said he would evaluate Shelley's skill level and make suggestions as to what training would be best for her. We made arrangements for Shelley to demonstrate her skills on the ice that Saturday.

When the day arrived, Shelley, Cathy and I met Ron at

the skating club. Ron took Shelley aside and talked with her for about thirty minutes. When they came back, Shelley was so excited. She said Ron wanted her to perform figures. Ron made a couple of corrections to Shelley's posture. They worked together for almost an hour. Shelley came back to the sidelines and changed to her free skates. For about an hour, she performed jumps and turns to music. After she came off the ice, Ron asked to speak to me privately. Meanwhile, the girls went off to explore the club's facilities.

Ron told me that even though Shelley had started late in skating, he believed she had the talent to skate at the international level. He said he would very much like to take Shelley on as a student. I told him I would get back to him after I had spoken to my husband and gotten his approval.

That evening I was listening to Joseph tell about his hockey game and how he had scored several goals. I asked Jerry how he had liked the game.

Oh, I didn't stay, he said, I had other things to do.

I decided it was time to talk about Shelley. I said that Ron thought that Shelley showed real promise as a skater.

Do what you want, Jerry said, indifferently. As long as you pay for it.

I was angry at his response and started saying so.

It's important that you support Shelley, I said.

I have to go out, Jerry said, cutting the conversation short. I'm meeting some people.

He got up and headed for the door.

I decided there was little to be gained by arguing. I would have to take care of this myself.

The next day I telephoned Ron and we agreed on the terms for coaching Shelley. That Saturday, Joseph, Cathy and I took Shelley to the club. When she was called out to skate, Shelley went through her figures effortlessly. She was given the highest marks for her fifth figure. On her sixth figure, Shelley skated gracefully and with total self-assurance. Shelley and Ron were called out on the ice for the results. Shelley had passed, not with the high marks she had earned on the fifth, but with a respectable standing. Shelley was flying high. Ron said how pleased he was with Shelley and the progress she had made. He said he would like to start working with Shelley on her free skate.

Shelley was beside herself with pride, and so were her mom and sister and brother.

Chapter Seventeen

It had been a few months since Jerry and I had last visited my mom. One Saturday we drove into Vancouver to visit her. When my mom answered the door, I was shocked. She must have weighed, at most, ninety pounds. My mom had always been a petite woman but she had never been as thin as this. She was really just skin and bone. Age had taken its toll on her but this was something more. I did not know what. My mom shuffled around the apartment, bent-over like a very old woman.

I told Jerry I was going for a walk to the corner store. There, I used the public telephone to call my mom's doctor. The doctor's opinion was that my mom needed proper nutrition and care. He informed me that my mom had not been eating. He said that Mom had a serious eating condition. She ate and then threw up. I was shocked.

The doctor advised me that, given my mom's eating habits, it would be little time before she died. I was in a dilemma as to what to do. Throughout my life, my mom had not cared for me in any real emotional way. But she had developed a strong relationship with Cathy. Could I leave her as she was, knowing it was only a matter of time before she died?

Certainly, we did not have the money to spend on professional care. If anyone was to care for my mom, it would have to be us.

Jerry and I decided to have my mom stay with us. Jerry took out her suitcase and packed a few of her things. He told her she was coming home with us. She objected, saying she was better off where she was. It was a half-hearted objection. She got up and put on her coat.

Come on, Mom, I'll help you, I said.

I went to take her arm. She pulled away from my grasp. She asked Jerry if he wouldn't mind helping her. She told me not to forget the suitcase.

Count to ten, I said to myself. Don't get mad. It won't help.

I kept quiet. Several thoughts were racing through my head.

What was I agreeing to? If this is how we were going to start off, what would it be like in a week's time, or even a month's? I thought, Maybe I should just run away, just walk out the door and not look back.

But I thought, She's your mom. You can't turn your back on her.

I picked up the suitcase. Once I was outside, I locked the door of the apartment behind me.

Jerry and my mom were already at the car.

I had about eight hundred dollars a month to pay for all our bills. My mom was not providing anything for the cost of staying with us—nor did I ask her to.

Christmas was almost upon us. I had no money to buy presents for the family or extra food for Christmas. I told Jerry that I needed more money for Christmas.

Forget it, he said. We're not having Christmas.

When you have kids, how can you not have Christmas? I demanded.

I don't care, he said. Do what you like.

I thought: what a jerk. I didn't dare ask my mom for any money for Christmas. I thought there should be something there for the kids on Christmas morning. They didn't have to be showered with gifts. We didn't even need a Christmas tree. But there should be something to mark the occasion.

It happened that I had a department charge account. My credit limit was something like a hundred dollars. About three weeks before Christmas, I got a letter from the department store saying my limit had been raised to one thousand dollars. It was part of a Christmas promotion.

I thought to myself, I'll use my card and I'll pay if off when the time comes.

And so I did. I bought some very inexpensive gifts for Jerry and the children and my mom, and some groceries, and a tree. We would have a very nice Christmas—not a huge Christmas—but a good one.

When Christmas Day arrived, everyone was pleased with their presents, including Jerry. I enjoyed seeing everyone so happy. Even my mom was more relaxed and appreciative. She did criticize me for not cooking the turkey the way she thought I should but I had made a decision that nothing was going to spoil our day. Halfway through the morning, Jerry said he was going out. When he announced his decision, I got upset with him.

It's Christmas, Jerry. It's time for families to be

together.

I just have to get out for a while, he replied.

But I've planned the day for us.

I'm going out, said Jerry. You have a good time without me. I'll be back in time for dinner.

He walked out the door.

A sadness fell over me. It really was sad that my husband did not want to stay home with his family on Christmas Day. I decided the day would not be ruined. I launched in and picked up where I had left off with my kids. We talked and laughed. Jerry had not spoiled Christmas for us, after all. Jerry arrived home about two hours before dinner, saying nothing about where he had been or what he had been doing.

I gave Jerry the receipts for the items I had bought at department and asked him to help pay for the Christmas expenses. His response was that it was my card and that I had made the decision to buy these things. Paying for them was my responsibility.

I felt I didn't have any other choice. I paid as fast and as much as I could. But it wasn't fast enough. I got a notice from the department store: the company would see me in court. When the day came, the lawyer who was acting on the department store's behalf raked me over the coals.

When it was my turn, I got up and told my story. My husband would not help me pay the bills for Christmas preparations and gifts. I had paid as much as I could. The judge was sympathetic. I was ordered to pay the amount of ten dollars a month. I paid it off as soon as I could.

I knew that Jerry had gotten the better of me. I didn't have the will to fight him—I think he knew that. He seemed to find more and more occasions to be purposely callous. I think he was hoping I would finally say I'd had enough of him. He seemed to be pushing me there. God knows I'd thought enough about leaving. What kind of marriage, after all, did we really have? I was hanging onto a thread and it was a pretty bare one.

But I was damned if I was going to walk out and jeopardize losing my family. And I was damned if I was going to make the decision for Jerry. If he was unhappy and wanted to leave, he was going to have to make that decision himself. In the meantime, I would take care of the things I could. I didn't need Jerry's support. God knows I'd been living without it for longer than I could remember.

Chapter Eighteen

As part of our consulting business, Jerry and I often filed documents at small claims court on behalf of our clients. I got to know Janice, the administrator there, quite well. We had many occasions to talk. One day, Janice informed me that there was an advertised opening for the position of Justice of the Peace.

What's a Justice of the Peace? I asked.

Janice said that in criminal court someone who has been accused must be seen by a Justice of the Peace within twenty-four hours of the arrest.

Sounds good to me, I said. What do I have to do?

Fill this in, she said, handing me an application form. Let me know when you get the job.

I was surprised and touched that Janice had such faith in me. For references, I put down the names of the Premier, and three members of the provincial legislature whom I considered my friends.

A couple weeks later, I was called to the Chief Judge's

office for an interview. Janice had told me to dress judicially, so I wore a black skirt, white blouse, a black jacket, black nylons and shoes. I figured that I looked very professional and as judicial as anyone could.

The Chief Judge's office was in the Toronto Dominion Tower in downtown Vancouver. Walking into the office, I was in no way prepared for what met my eyes. The wooden furnishings were very elaborate and the carpet so thick I could have lain down on it. People walked about speaking in hushed tones. Even their footsteps were whispers.

I was ushered into a boardroom with the largest table I have ever seen. Then, the Chief Judge came in and we chatted for a few minutes. He invited me into his office for the formal interview and looked over my application.

Well, we can't very well call the Premier of the province, can we? he said, looking up from my application.

Why not? I asked. I have his cell number. I could telephone him right now, if you like.

No, that won't be necessary, the Chief Judge said.

We talked for the next hour. I asked a lot of questions about the position of Justice of the Peace. I really did not have any idea what was expected and what a Justice's duties, in fact, were. The Chief Judge was very deliberate in answering every one of my questions. With each answer, another question popped into my head.

At the end of the hour the Chief Judge showed me around the office and introduced me to each person who was working there.

Well, this is different, I thought to myself.

There were several other judges in the outer office at the time and the Chief Judge led me out and introduced me to them. I chatted with each of them for several minutes. I was wondering whether this was part of the interview. Maybe the Chief Judge wanted to see just how nervous I was or how well I handled talking to others.

We went back into the boardroom and had coffee. I felt very much at ease with the Chief Judge. We finally shook hands and said our goodbyes. The Chief Judge said it was very nice meeting me and that he was sure we would meet again soon. My response was that I had really enjoyed meeting him and the other judges and everyone in the office and I hoped I would get the opportunity to meet with them again.

The Chief Judge advised me that he would let me know very soon.

As it was, I did not have to wait very long for his reply. Less than a week later, I received a letter from the Chief Judge's office requesting me to return. The letter said I had been accepted for the position of Justice of the Peace.

The next Monday, at two o'clock in the afternoon, I again appeared in the Chief Judge's office. The furnishings appeared to be just as elaborate as they had on my first visit, the carpet just as deep. This time, though, the greeting was much different than before. There was no formality. It was: Hi, Colleen. I'm glad to see you. Come in and make yourself comfortable. Coffee?

Yes, black, please, I said.

I stood in awe of my surroundings, the dusty rose carpet and the cherry wood furniture that had been polished within an inch of its life.

This time we sat together in the boardroom and the Chief Judge showed me a copy of the Criminal Code of Canada and an outline of my duties. This time, I really was nervous. The realization settled on me that as a Justice of the Peace I would have the freedom of others in my hands.

The Chief Judge seemed to sense my misgivings. He

asked me if I was feeling nervous. I admitted that I was—not nervous about the position—but nervous about having the fate of people in my hands. The Chief Judge smiled and assured me that after my first few times in court, the feeling would go away.

The Chief Judge mentioned that he had called the Premier and that the Premier had given me the highest recommendation. He said I would receive training for my position through the Justice Institute of British Columbia and that a stringent examination would follow. If I was successful with the examination, I would be sworn in as a Justice of the Peace.

I was so excited I could hardly contain myself. When I walked out of the Chief Judge's office, I can say I did not feel the carpet under my feet. I stepped out onto the sidewalk. The noise of the traffic going by was abrupt and loud. Cars and people rushed by on either side. Had I been dreaming? No, it seemed I hadn't been. I saw myself reflected in the glass of a building: a woman dressed in black skirt and jacket, and soon to be a Justice of the Peace.

On a Monday morning in November I arrived at the Justice Institute of British Columbia. The grounds were beautifully groomed with large trees all around and beautiful flowers.

I have to admit I was very nervous. I took a deep breath and got up enough nerve to walk inside. Right inside the door was the receptionist. She looked up and smiled at me and I smiled back. I told her my name and the reason I was there. She took out an identification tag for me to wear and instructed me on how to get to my classroom.

This building was a far cry from the Chief Judge's office. It looked more like a barracks. There were many police officers in uniform and some, I guessed, in plain clothes.

I arrived at my classroom and I found there were ten of us taking the class. Of the ten, eight were court clerks being upgraded to Justices of the Peace. One other person and myself were new bees, so to speak.

Our instructor was a Justice of the Peace, by the name of Daniel Reader. Daniel had worked in the judicial system for many years and was very knowledgeable. For the first hour and a half he spoke to the group in general about the duties of a Justice of the Peace. Daniel advised us that we would all be lay Justices of the Peace. We were not lawyers. Nor did we have any formal training in the law. Daniel also advised us that we were not to expect to catch on to everything right away but we would learn as we did our duties. For the next hour or so he spoke alone to the two of us who were new and gave us an orientation to the judicial system.

Lunch time came and we all went into the cafeteria. I had never seen so many police officers in one place. There was one man whom I couldn't help noticing. He was tall and extremely thin. He wore jeans and a tee shirt and a sleeveless jean jacket. He had grey hair and it was tied back in a long ponytail. It was so long it extended past his waist.

Daniel noticed my attention was focused elsewhere.

You find him interesting? he asked.

I said, Daniel, I thought we were in the prestigious Justice Institute. What's that man doing here?

Daniel started to laugh.

Colleen, he's an undercover officer. They're supposed to look like that.

I was embarrassed that I had been so naïve.

Don't worry, Daniel said, still laughing. You'll soon learn.

Our course went on and it proved challenging—at least, to the two of us who were new. We learned about search warrants, the how to's and the not to's. We learned about the Family Relations Act and the Canada Evidence Act. We learned that an "Information" is the first document you see with the charges against the alleged accused on it, and how to process the document. We underwent a number of mock court hearings to learn the correct procedures and the pitfalls we might encounter and how to be wary of them. We scrutinized our Justice of the Peace manual and the Criminal Code of Canada. These would be our bibles, so to speak.

We spent a full day on search warrants. We learned what to expect, what to accept, and what not to accept; what reasonable and probable grounds are to issue a search warrant; and how to judge whether a police officer had a satisfactory reason for a search warrant to be issued.

We were taught to make our decisions about each case very carefully but very quickly. You might have close to a hundred cases in one day to decide upon. You couldn't be swayed by a lawyer's arguments. You had to the listen to the evidence and make up your own mind

We also learned that Crown Counsel had better be ready with all the details of the case. If Crown was asking for a detention order and didn't have the documents to back it up, most likely the alleged accused would walk.

The day of our exam arrived. My head was in a whirl. I was scared. Would I be able to meet the requirements, and then, sit in a courtroom and render judgments? Would I have the confidence to issue a search warrant and be sure all the i's were dotted and all the t's were crossed? I could only do my best.

We sat down to the exam. There were questions on all the aspects we had learned. When out time was up, we were excused to go for coffee. The exams were to be marked while we waited for the results. All ten of us were very quiet, waiting for the axe to fall.

We were called back into the classroom and the results given. I wasn't prepared for the report. I had achieved the highest mark: ninety nine and one half percent.

I was a little shocked. I sat, not able to say a word. The adjudicator called each of us to the front of the class to be congratulated. He called me first, saying that he wanted to recognize my excellent results. Our marks would be sent to the Chief Judge's office. When it was time, each of us would be called before the Administrative Judge in our area and sworn in as a Justice of the Peace.

That afternoon, as I left, I looked back at the building and the beautiful lawn and the flowers. I wanted to take it all in. I felt a new era in my life was about to begin.

I called home and told Jerry that I had done really well on my exam. I told him my mark. Would he like to get together for dinner and celebrate?

He said he had other things to do.

I was hurt, and angry.

What other things? I asked.

He stammered and wouldn't answer. I told him I would be home by about eight. He said he wouldn't be home until later.

When I got home that night, I sat down with my mom and told her what I had accomplished. I told her I had gotten the highest mark and that I was going to be a Justice of the Peace.

Is that so? she said. A Justice of the Peace. Well, now that you're home, I wouldn't mind a cup of coffee.

I phoned my Aunt Gail and Uncle Ray and told them the news and they were happy and said they were proud of me.

Uncle Ray kept saying, Here comes the judge, here comes the judge.

I laughed and said, Oh, Uncle Ray.

He said, Honestly, Colleen, we are so very proud of what you have accomplished.

Cathy, Shelley and Joseph were happy for me, too.

We'll have to be good, Joseph joked, now that Mom's on the bench.

When Jerry came home, I told him about my new position.

That's nice, he said.

One day I received a call from the nurse at Joseph's school.

What's the problem, I asked. Don't tell me he's hurt himself somehow.

No, that's not the problem. It's been reported that your son is undernourished.

You're joking, I said.

No, not all. I'm told he isn't bringing lunch to school.

Have you ever seen my son?

No, she said.

My temper flared.

My son has a lunch for him every day, I said. And, if he forgets it at home, then he will eat it when he gets home from school. And, before you make accusations like this, you had better check out the situation. My son is five foot ten and weighs a hundred and seventy pounds. He plays defense in football and he's a defenseman on the hockey team.

I could hear her taking a deep breath.

Don't ever call me again like this, I said. Or I'll have you fired.

Soon after, I got a telephone call from the Chief Judge's office directing me to contact the Administrative Judge in my area. I was to be sworn in as a Justice of the Peace. When I got off the phone, I sat and cried. I felt tremendous joy and wonderment at the news. I said: Colleen O'Connor, Justice of the Peace for the Province of British Columbia. That was my title. It was going to take some getting used to.

I called Aunty Gail and Uncle Ray first. They both were excited. Then I called the Premier on his cell. I thanked him for the reference he had given.

You deserve it, Colleen, he said, laughing. You deserve it—and more. Had you been a lawyer, I'd have recommended you as a judge.

I said, Thank you. My face is redder than my hair.

Why don't you come to the island? he said. We'll have dinner with a few of your friends to celebrate.

I will, I said. Just let me know when it's convenient.

I'll do that, he said. Congratulations, Colleen. I'm proud of you.

I started to cry.

I'll see you soon, the Premier said.

Yes, soon, I said, and hung up the phone.

Cathy, Shelley and Joseph came to see me sworn in. The ceremony was held in the Judge's private chambers. The room was beautifully furnished and the carpets were like those in the Chief Judge's office—very plush and deep. The furniture was cherry wood.

The Judge advised me that my oath was more important than a marriage ceremony. He said that it was a commitment of the highest order. Then I was sworn in.

I signed the documents and was given my copy. Then all of us we went into the open courtroom. The Judge brought me up to the front of the courtroom and introduced me as the newest Justice of the Peace for the Province of British Columbia.

When we were done, I took all my children and hugged them tight. I had tears of joy.

We all took a walk around the courthouse and the police station.

I said, Well, I guess this is going to be my home away from home.

At the time, I didn't know just how true that was.

I had been directed to contact a Justice of the Peace in my area. His name was Pete. He was to act as my mentor. Pete was a retired Royal Canadian Mounted Police Inspector. I made arrangements to meet with him while he was on duty and to sit in with him. That day we signed four search warrants, one to search for horses, and three to search for drugs.

At the end of the day, Pete said he was not going to be available that evening and asked whether I could stand in as Justice of the Peace. I said yes, never thinking I would be called.

Right after dinner, the telephone rang. It was a police officer, wanting a search warrant, in regard to a sexual assault.

I phoned Pete.

Can I do this? I asked.

Of course, you can, said Pete. Go for it. Just don't let anybody lead you down the garden path. Remember: who, what, where, when and how.

In a very short time, two officers in uniform arrived at my house.

You're new, said the officer whom I met at the door. He eyed his partner and smiled.

I tried to be professional and not let on about my inexperience. I sent the children down to watch television. I took the officers into the kitchen. They handed me the warrant.

The information they gave me was related to a terrible sexual assault. The more details I read, the redder my face got.

The police officers just grinned at me.

From the particulars in the report I decided there were adequate grounds for issuing a warrant. At the kitchen table, I signed my first document as a Justice of the Peace.

My married life was getting worse. Jerry continued to say cruel things and put me down. He said no man would ever want me. It got to the point that when he started in on me, I couldn't hear what he was saying. It was as if I was in another world. It got easier and easier for me to do.

It never crossed my mind that Jerry might be jealous of me becoming a Justice, but now, when I look back, I think that was the case.

My mom was losing weight and at the same time refusing to eat. She had difficulty breathing. The doctor said she would need to go into long-term care. It was clear that she was getting weaker. Fortunately, we were able to find a facility to take her.

Aunty Gail and Uncle Ray kept me sane. We called each other almost every day. Sometimes I would cry out of frustration and hurt. Uncle Ray assured me that this difficult time would pass. Both my aunt and uncle said not to let the frustrations of my life get me down. Uncle Ray asked why I wasn't packing my bags and leaving Jerry.

I said I was afraid of losing what family I had. I couldn't handle risking that all over again.

It was getting harder for me to attend to the business that Jerry and I owned. I had worked very hard to make it successful and felt I was working without Jerry's support. The atmosphere at the office was strained. I was in constant disagreements with Jody, an employee whom I learned was collecting assistance benefits while she was working in our office. I had a low opinion of anyone who took advantage of a system meant to help those in a jam.

One day, I felt I had had enough. After another argument with Jody, I was steaming.

Look, you fraud, I shouted, get out of my office and don't come back.

She took off in a huff.

When Jerry found out what I had done, he hit me hard across the face and walked out of the office. I told our employees to go home early for the night and I shut the office. I called Aunty Gail and told her what had happened.

Pack his clothes and kick him out, she said. Don't let him back in the house.

How can I do that to the kids? I asked.

Just do it, she said.

Jerry came home and the evening was horrible, with Jerry calling me everything under the sun and hitting me again. I went into my own world. He could yell at me all he wanted. I could not hear him.

Chapter Nineteen

I was a Justice of the Peace; I was operating a business, and taking care of my mom and my kids. I was busy. In the meantime, time passed. My children were growing up.

When Joseph was sixteen years old, I got a telephone call one night from the police. The constable on the telephone was laughing. He asked if I had a son by the name of Joseph. I said yes. The officer said he said he was taking Joseph to the hospital and for me to meet him there. He said I didn't have to worry. Joseph wasn't in any danger. He wouldn't say anything more.

When I got to the emergency room, I found Joseph covered in blood from head to toe.

What in heaven's name happened? I asked the officer.

The officer told me that Joseph had found out his girlfriend was cheating on him; he had been drinking, and had tripped over the street curb. He had fallen head-first into a plate-glass window and smashed it to pieces. The officer said that he had asked Joseph his name. The officer had recognized it right away as mine. He said he picked Joseph up like a kitten and shook him and told him that if he ever got into trouble again he would not know what happened to him.

From that date on, Joseph was a well behaved young man. If he did get into trouble, it never reached my ears.

In the meantime, Shelley had given up figure skating, even though she had placed high in the standings. She had broken her ankle and this had convinced her that she would never be strong enough to do as well as she hoped. Shelley had decided on horses as a second choice and was learning to ride and to train.

Shelley met a young man by the name of Roger and in a very short time they decided to get married. Roger was in construction and had aspirations to be a superintendent. He was absolutely fond of Shelley and treated her like a princess. He had a house in south Surrey where they moved to after their wedding. I was so happy that Shelley had found someone who cared for her.

Meanwhile, my mom had taken sick. She was having more difficulty breathing. The doctor ordered her into the hospital. She had lost more weight, was barely sixty-five pounds. Her intake of food had dropped to little more than a little cheese, and water. The doctor prepared me for the worst. He said he believed that Mom no longer had the will to live—or to get better. We made arrangements for my mom to go into hospital.

One morning, I was dragging my heels before work. I knew I would have to deal with another day of Jerry's indifference. I was sitting outside on the back steps of the house with a cup of coffee and talking to our cat, Missy, when the telephone rang. I grudgingly went into the kitchen to answer it.

A woman's voice at the other end of the telephone asked, Is this Colleen O'Connor?

Yes, I said.

Hi, Mom. This is Arlene.

Is this some kind of joke? I said.

This is no joke, the woman said. Mom, it's Arlene. Your daughter. Arlene.

I took a long deep breath and then I began to cry.

How did you find me? I asked.

Arlene said she had been taken to the eye doctor years before and that she had been called into the office by the name, Arlene O'Connor. When the doctor had stepped out, leaving her for a minute, she had peeked at her file and read the names, Colleen and Jerry O'Connor. She said she had kept the names to herself for years. She had searched the telephone directory and had found Jerry's name.

We talked for a long time. Then, Arlene said she had to go. I had to be at work myself. I promised her I would call her later that night.

When I got to work, I found Cathy helping out. Jerry was angry that I was late. I said I had had enough for the day. I told Cathy that I would see her at home.

I drove to the beach and went for a long walk. I found a place to sit. I watched the boats and listened to the waves lapping onto the shore. It was a warm spring day filled with sunshine. I took off my shoes and walked in the water. I came to a very secluded spot where it was shady but warm. I sat down on a log to think about everything that had happened that day. When I next looked at my watch, it was almost three hours later.

That night Arlene and I spoke again and on several occasions over the next few weeks. We both decided that we wanted to meet, and to see where that might lead.

The day I was to meet Arlene for the first time happened to be the day after my mom went into hospital. In the morning I called and talked to the nurse. She said my mom's condition was no worse and not to worry. I hung up the phone and headed out the door.

I took the helijet to Victoria. Arlene met me at the airport. I knew her right away. She was standing outside of the terminal when I disembarked. Arlene was a tall, pretty, young woman, very slender, with blondish-brown hair.

Colleen! She said.

Yes, Arlene, I said.

We hugged.

Our first meeting was strained and difficult for us both. There had been so many years intervening. We had some lunch and talked. We tried to catch up on all the events that had transpired in our lives, and that had been lost to each other. Arlene said she was married but was separated. She was in the process of getting a divorce. She was working and taking courses to further her career as a credit manager. I told her I was very pleased that she was doing so well.

But I was feeling increasingly frustrated and angry as Arlene told the story she had come to hear about our separation: that I had abandoned her and that I had not been able to care for her. I tried to convince Arlene that she had never been abandoned, that she had been loved from the very moment she came into the world and that she had been nothing less than a joy to me. But our conversation was difficult. It seemed to me that Arlene could not believe what I was saying.

The time came for my flight back to the mainland. Arlene and I said goodbye. I told her we would get together soon and that I would call her in the next few days.

I arrived back at the hospital at three o'clock in the

afternoon. Cathy was there to meet me.

Where were you, Mom? she said. Grandma's not doing well.

I gave some excuse as to why I was late.

When I went into my mom's room, she was already in a coma. Her breathing was short and difficult. Cathy and I sat by her bed.

Shelley, her husband, Roger, and Joseph came to the hospital at five o'clock. One of the nurses asked to meet with us in another room. There she told us my mom was not going to make it through the night. She asked if we wanted my mom resuscitated, if need be. I said I believed my mom had had enough of this world. I said we did not have the right to insist on her being somewhere she did not want to be.

How much time does she have? I asked.

Not much time, the nurse said. Maybe a couple of hours.

With that news, I felt the tears on my face. I told the kids that we needed to go back to my mom's room and be with her. This was not a time for her to be alone.

Do you think she knows we're here? I asked the nurse.

I don't think so, she replied. You might want to talk to her anyway. Tell her it's all right to leave this world and that you care for her.

Is she in pain? I asked. If she is, I want her given medication for it.

No, the nurse assured me. She's in no pain.

We went back to Mom's room and stood by her bed. I held her hand, on one side, and Shelley, Joseph, and Cathy stood on the other side, just touching her hand.

Suddenly, Mom took a deep breath. We all knew what was happening. Roger looked at me with tears in his eyes.

She's gone, he said sadly.

At that moment I saw an iridescent light come from my mom's body. It was in the shape of a head and it had a smile. At that moment, Cathy looked at me.

Don't cry, Mom, she said. Grandma's smiling at us.

Then, the iridescent light disappeared.

In a short time, a doctor came and pronounced Mom deceased. The nurse took the breathing apparatus away. A priest gave Mom the last rites.

Before the nurse left, I told her what Cathy and I had experienced.

You're very privileged, the nurse said. You saw her soul leaving her body. It's very rare to see it happen.

When we got back from the hospital, Jerry was home.

I said to him, Mom just passed on.

He said, Well, it's about time.

He crawled into bed.

I went into the hall and cried. I thought about my mom and how much I had wanted to be loved by her. I thought about Arlene and how I had not been able to know her as a daughter. Then and there I decided it was time that my three children finally knew: they had two sisters and a brother they had never met.

It was late but I had to talk to Uncle Ray and Aunty Gail. I called them in Calgary. When I told them of Mom's death, they said they would leave the next morning in order to be with me. We talked for a long time. I told Aunt Gail how Jerry had responded to the news that Mom had died.

Well, that's to be expected from Jerry, she said.

What do you mean?

One day soon you'll find out, she said finally. I'll see you tomorrow.

The next day Cathy, Shelley and I went to Memorial Gardens and made the arrangements for the funeral. My aunt and uncle arrived later that evening. My cousin, Mike, had come in from the island. Later, Jerry showed up without any word as to where he had been or why he was arriving so late. As soon as he walked in, I could feel the friction in the room. I don't think any words passed between Jerry and my aunt and uncle. Mike looked as if he was about to say a word to Jerry but didn't. Mike turned his back to him.

The day of the funeral I went to the funeral home on my own. I didn't know where Jerry was. All I could say when I was asked was that I didn't know where he might be. There were about twenty-five of us, mostly family and our friends. Jerry came in, finally.

When the service was about to begin, I walked in with my children and with my aunt and uncle by my side. I suddenly lost any composure I had. I became hysterical, not on account of my mom but because of everything inside me. I had been holding onto my feelings and keeping them to myself. Aunty Gail and Uncle Ray took me into another room. They held me between them and let me cry.

We all went to Shelley's house after the service. I was glad to see everyone, especially Mike whom I had not seen since I had lived on the island. When everyone left Shelley's, I helped clean up and put things away. My aunt and uncle stayed behind and we sat and talked the rest of the evening, mostly about my mom.

The next morning, my aunt and uncle left for Calgary. The very next afternoon following their departure, the doorbell rang. I went to answer the door and was met by Aunty Gail and Uncle Ray. I asked them what in the world they were doing back in town.

They explained they had gotten home, repacked their bags with clean clothes, and driven back that morning. When Jerry arrived home that night, it was obvious he was not pleased to see Gail or Ray. He walked in, said he had other things to do, and walked out again.

The next day, as my aunt and uncle and I were chatting, my Aunt Gail asked whether I had seen any of my other children. The question stopped me dead in my tracks. I had not told anyone that I had met Arlene.

Yes, I said, finally. I've seen Arlene.

I told how Arlene had been able to identify Jerry and myself as her parents and how she had contacted me. Aunty Gail asked me if I had told anyone. I said I hadn't for fear of reprisal from Jerry. And, as much as I wanted, I hadn't felt ready to tell my other children that they had two sisters and a brother whom they knew nothing of.

I want you to listen, said my Aunt Gail. There are a few things you don't know. They should have been told you a long time ago. As much as you've wanted children, that's never been the case with Jerry. We know for a fact that Jerry paid his friends to report you to welfare.

I didn't say a word. I don't know if I could have at that moment. I just sat dumbfounded.

Aunty Gail was saying, The first child was the hardest to convince welfare—that you were ignoring her and being negligent. Your second child was easy. Jerry's friends said they lived close to you and that they could hear the baby crying night and day.

I was trembling. Aunty Gail went on.

As for your third baby, Jerry was the one who arranged for his friends to take her. Bringing her to the welfare office was planned before you'd even left for Long Beach. The couple did what Jerry told them. They reported the baby abandoned two days after you'd gone. They told the welfare office you'd asked them to baby-sit for a few hours—and that you never returned.

I sat in disbelief at what I was hearing.

This can't be true, I said.

My Aunt Gail had tears in her eyes.

I'm afraid it is, she said.

How do you know?

Mike found out. He's the one who tracked it down. He was in the service, and he went around asking questions.

Is there any proof? I asked.

He told Jerry that he knew what he had been up to. Jerry just laughed at him. He told Mike he'd better keep his mouth shut—or he'd be dead.

I shook my head.

It can't be true, I said. Jerry can be mean, but he's always loved me.

Colleen, said Aunty Gail, Jerry's been cheating on you all along.

Since when?

The words out of my mouth were just a whisper.

Since the day you were married, said Aunty Gail. Stop and think about where he goes when he leaves the house. Does he ever tell you where he is going or when he's coming back? And, for that matter, does he ever invite you to join him?

I sat still. I had had my suspicions.

You've proof? I said.

Call Mike, Aunty Gail said, touching my hand. He'll tell you.

Would you? I asked.

I was trembling. Aunty Gail went to the phone and called Mike's number.

Mike, I heard her say, it's Gail. I've told Colleen everything you've told me. She'd like to talk to you.

She handed me the phone.

Mike? I said.

Hi, Colleen.

Mike, tell me it's not true. Tell me it wasn't Jerry who reported me to welfare.

I can't do that, Colleen. I wish I could. It's all true— every bit of it.

You're sure?

Yeah, I'm sure. I'm sorry.

Me, too.

Colleen, I'm sorry I didn't have the courage to tell you.

I understand, I said.

I was crying.

Mike, was Jerry having affairs on me all this time?

Yeah, with anybody he could.

That's why there's been bad blood between you?

Yeah, you could say that.

Thanks, Mike. I'll call you . . . once I get this sorted out.

You do that, he said. Bye, Colleen.

I put the phone down. I was trembling like a leaf in a storm. Uncle Ray held me.

My aunt and uncle and I met Nancy and Gillian the next day for dinner. I told them about what I had learned from Aunty Gail and that Mike had verified it.

Gillian told of an occasion when Jerry had propositioned her. Gillian had a son who skated with our Joseph. Sometimes, at the skating rink Jerry would come over to where Gillian was sitting and they would chat and have coffee. One time

Jerry asked Gillian out for a bite to eat. She accepted. She saw nothing wrong in getting together for dinner. By the time the meal was over, Jerry had asked her to have an affair with him. She said she had been shocked. She told him where to go and how to get there. She had asked him how he could do this to me. His response was that no man would touch me. Gillian tossed her glass of water in Jerry's face before getting up and walking out.

Nancy had a similar story. She said Jerry had invited her to meet him when he was visiting in Vancouver. When she had gotten to the meeting, Jerry had made a wild pass at her. Nancy had told him that she was not going to have anything to do with him.

Nancy declared a toast to me, and everyone at the table raised their glasses.

To Colleen, she proclaimed, to the next part of her life.

There was great cry of acclamation all around.

I know you have the courage to see this through, said Nancy.

I hope so, I said.

Aunty Gail and Uncle Ray assured me they were there for me any time I needed them. Nancy and Gillian chimed in their support as well. But I was not sure. I had a lot to think about. This had all come too quickly. I had had no time to consider my options.

You might want to talk to Cathy, my Aunt Gail suggested. She will understand. She can be there for you.

I said that I would confide in Cathy when the time was right but that I was not going to say anything to Jerry for the moment.

I was going to wait and see what I might do.

When Jerry came home that night, he was in a terrible mood.

No man will ever touch you, he said. Who would want you?

You shouldn't throw rocks at glass houses. Your house is shattering, I shot back.

Your aunt and uncle aren't welcome in this house.

Just try and stop them from coming in to my house ever, I answered. You'll have the police to deal with.

Jerry walked out the door.

As the door slammed closed, I shouted, Don't come back.

The following Saturday afternoon was a beautiful day. There wasn't a cloud in the sky. It was sunny and warm for the end of April. I called Cathy and asked her if she would meet me at my mom's grave site. She said she would.

Within a minute of our arriving, a flash thunderstorm suddenly rolled in. A bolt of lightning came down a short distance from us. It was enough to make us jump. We agreed we had better find shelter at my house.

The thunderstorm seemed to follow us. As soon as we made it to the house, the storm went on its way.

I made Cathy a rum and coke, a very strong rum and coke.

I want you to sit down, I said. I have to tell you something I've kept from you for a long time.

Cathy did as she was asked.

What's this about? she said.

Cathy, I said, you have two sisters and a brother you've never met.

She looked at me incredulously. I told her the whole

story, including what I had learned through Aunty Gail and Mike. I said I had met Arlene only a few days before. I told Cathy as much as I knew about her sister.

Are you sure of all of this? she asked.

Yes, I said. I know this is all a surprise. For twenty years, I've wanted to tell you the truth but I didn't have the courage.

Cathy had a couple more drinks. She was in shock. I gave Arlene's phone number to her. Cathy said she was going right home to telephone Arlene. She was in tears. The news I had given her had been completely unexpected.

Cathy telephoned me early the next day. She told me that Arlene and she had talked for hours, catching up on the events that had happened in their separate lives.

Now it was Cathy's turn to surprise me. Cathy said that Arlene had learned that Sarah was living on Vancouver Island. Sarah's last name was Turner. Arlene had even known Sarah in school but had had no idea that they were sisters. She said Sarah and she had met at school and gotten to be friends. Neither had any intimation of their shared past. She said often people would comment on how alike they looked.

Arlene and Cathy made arrangements to meet. Cathy decided she was determined to find Sarah. She wrote a letter that said she was looking for her sister, Sarah Turner, who lived on the island. She copied it one hundred times and sent it to everyone on the island named Turner. I was happy she was doing this—not for my sake—but for hers. She wanted very much to meet Sarah. It became her mission and I wished her all the luck in her quest.

Cathy received plenty of responses to her letter. They were people wishing her luck and hoping that she would be successful finding her sister. On Thanksgiving evening,

Cathy received a telephone call.

Is this Cathy? asked the woman on the other end of the line.

Yes, Cathy said.

Hi, Cathy. This is your sister, Sarah.

Cathy burst into tears. So did Sarah. They talked well into the night. Before they hung up, they agreed on a date for them to meet on the island.

Cathy called me and was very excited about her success in finding Sarah and having talked to her. She gave me Sarah's number. I swallowed and called the number. Sarah answered. We talked for a long time. I learned that she had just spoken to Arlene. Sarah was married and had five children of her own. She was twenty-four.

I told her of my memories of her as a baby and included what I had learned just recently about Jerry's part in her apprehension. Sarah said I must be mistaken about the details. She said her adoptive parents had told her that they had met Jerry and that he had been quite a concerned young father.

I didn't know what I could say to counter what Sarah had learned as a child. I suggested that she and Arlene telephone Auntie Gail and Uncle Ray in Alberta. Sarah asked me what I did for a living. I told her I was a Justice of the Peace in criminal court and explained what I did.

We agreed that we should meet but left the time and the place for a meeting up in the air. Both of us were uncomfortable and awkward during our conversation.

I was grasping at ways we might move our conversation forward. Here the two of us were, with quite different accounts of the past, and little option to bridge them. I understood something about Sarah's predicament: she had a story of the past that she took to be the truth, and was hesitant to give it up. So, too had I. I had been living for the longest time with a story I had tried to understand as best I could. I had found the story to have been terribly incomplete. I felt deeply Sarah's distrust of me.

Could she really believe what I was saying? Could she give up one story which she had learned to be "true" for another she was not sure about? It was no wonder that our conversation seemed to stall, sputter, and go nowhere. I put the phone down feeling more dissatisfied than ever. I suspected Sarah felt much the same.

It took a very short time for Jerry to learn that I had met Arlene and spoken with Sarah. Cathy was thrilled that she had found her two sisters and that her search for Sarah had been successful. I had expected that Cathy would share the discovery with Jerry, and with her friends.

But I was far from ready to broach the subject of my meeting Arlene with Jerry. I could no longer trust Jerry, and I did not know what he might do with any information I might give him. I was unsure myself what to do next.

I set myself a plan, of sorts. It was August. I was leaving for Alberta. Aunt Gail and Uncle Ray's daughter, Elizabeth, was getting married. I decided that the day of my flight I would confront Jerry. The thought of doing so scared me half to death. But I knew it couldn't wait any longer.

The afternoon of my flight, I brought down my luggage to the front door. Jerry happened to be in the kitchen. I went in. Jerry was pouring himself some coffee.

I'm leaving for the airport, I said. But before I do, I have to tell you something.

Jerry didn't seemed interested.

What is it? he asked.

After all these years, I've found out you're the one responsible for welfare being called, and for the kids being taken.

He smirked, and then laughed.

You don't know what you're talking about.

I do know, I said. How could you, Jerry?

He started his usual diatribe: I was not worth anything. It was no wonder no man would touch me.

I stayed as calm as I could.

I'm going, I said. I want you out of my life—and out of here—by the time I get back.

Jerry struck me, and started to walk away.

But I hadn't finished.

You are a liar and a cheat, and you wouldn't know the truth if you fell over it. You've lived nothing but a lie all your life. You've pulled me down to your level. But it will never happen again. I've learned a hard lesson, but it's one I'll never forget.

Jerry was already heading out the door.

I called Cathy and asked if she would pick me up at the airport when I returned Sunday night. I told her that I had confronted her dad. She asked me if I was sure about what I was doing.

I've had my fill living a terrible lie, I said.

At that moment Jerry came back into the house.

I said, Don't forget I want you out of this house when I come home on Sunday. You can leave the house keys with Cathy.

I'm sure that Jerry heard me. But he didn't stop. He went upstairs. I heard the door slam closed.

When I arrived in Alberta, Uncle Ray met me at the airport. Seeing him, I felt as though I was coming home. Uncle Ray and I talked and teased each other all the way from the airport. Aunt Gail and Uncle Ray's home was modest, but comfortable. There was a dining room table, the kind you see in old farmhouses, that you pull open and that seats as many as twelve. When we arrived, Aunty Gail had dinner on the table. There were ten or so of us. My cousins had arrived, and their families. We laughed and talked and joked.

Even though it was their daughter's wedding, that evening Aunt Gail and Uncle Ray wouldn't let me raise a finger to help. I felt completely spoiled. We all got up early the next day and got the house ready for the ceremony. It was an outside wedding to be held in my aunt and uncle's back yard. That meant putting up the decorations and laying out the table covers and the table centerpieces.

Uncle Ray was in a teasing mood. We spent a good part of the day tossing remarks to each other and laughing. When the time came for the wedding, I found a seat a few rows back. But Uncle Ray would have none of that. He took me by the arm and accompanied me to the front row where the rest of his and Aunty Gail's family was sitting.

You'll sit right here, he said. You're family.

And he gave me a hug.

It was a sunny day, perfect for a wedding. I remember my aunt and uncle sitting together in the sunlight while their daughter exchanged her vows with her husband to be. It was a special moment for them, with their friends and family gathered around them. That Sunday I spent the whole day with my aunt and uncle. We picked up after the wedding celebration and found occasions to talk and laugh.

When it came time for me to return home, I felt sick thinking about what I faced ahead of me. On the plane home, huge butterflies tumbled about in my stomach.

When I got off the plane and walked down the ramp, I saw Cathy and Shelley waiting for me. I asked where Jerry was. They said he had moved out on the weekend to his girl friend's house. As soon as I heard this, my stomach settled and I was fine. The girls and I went home and we talked most of the night. Cathy stayed with me that night after Shelley went home. I was scared and unsure of what my next step might be.

I don't think I can make it, I said to Cathy. I really don't.

You'll be fine, she assured me. You have made it this far. You will make it the rest of the way.

I just sobbed my heart out, not because of Jerry, but because I was now alone and had no idea where to turn.

Then, within my mind (at the time I could not explain it) I heard the most beautiful sound. It was a bird singing a song of love and caring. It was my Phoenix singing to me. He was sending his hot tears to make me feel better. He was delivering his song to my heart to give me strength.

And he continued to do so, over the next days and weeks.

I phoned Aunt Gail and Uncle Ray and told them that Jerry and I were no longer together. They both seemed to breathe a sigh of relief.

Now, you start living your life, Aunt Gail said to me. Start enjoying it.

How can I think of that, I asked, when I'm feeling so bad?

Aunt Gail was sympathetic.

That's just the shock of not having to answer to anyone except yourself, she said.

We talked for a long time. After we had finished and I had put the phone down, I heard again the wonderful song of the Phoenix. He was singing to me and sending me strength to carry on.

Chapter Twenty

My work as a Justice of the Peace helped me get my mind off my personal life. I immersed myself in work. I realized I loved doing my court work. I looked forward every day to getting to court.

My right hand man was a staff sergeant but most people referred to him as a tough cop. He had operated undercover in the drug world for a very long time. He was tall, thin, and bowlegged. He had a rugged face weathered by life's experiences. He could call a spade a spade. On the occasions he disagreed with my decisions Sarge would address me as "Madame" and would speak to me in a disapproving way. Whenever that happened, I would ask myself what I had done to raise his ire and reevaluate what I had said or done. Sometimes I would just shrug my shoulders and say, Oh well, too bad, my decision.

That year we had a full-blown snowstorm. Snow had fallen through the evening and promised to do the same throughout the day. I got to court. We had a full slate and worked into the afternoon. I was tired when court was over. Sarge came into the court room and handed me a cup of steaming coffee. I was ever so grateful. We sat and talked. He said that he heard a rumor that I had separated from my husband.

I said, You heard correct.

If you ever need just to talk, he said, I'm here. You know you're a damn good Justice.

I said, Thank you very much. I really appreciate it.

I happened to meet Vivian Woods, also a redhead, who worked as credit manager for a large firm. She and I became good friends. I found a house to buy in town that had a full suite in the basement. The very first person I asked to move in was Vivian. She jumped at the chance.

Sometimes we would have dinner together, either one of us deciding to cook. Often, when I was on duty, it was not surprising to have a few police officers to the house to ask me to sign warrants. Often they would stay and chat. It wasn't unusual for them to walk in the door and ask if the coffee was on.

After Vivian and I had been sharing the house for several months, we decided to go to the greatest little city in the world, Reno, just the two of us. When the members of the police force heard of our plans, they laughingly threatened to keep a watch on us. Their Justice of the Peace and her friend were going to be out on the town. The greatest little city in the world wouldn't be safe with the two of us there.

Vivian and I, two women separated from our husbands, flew into the town on the weekend of Valentine's Day. As we were about to disembark, three police officers boarded the plane. There was some consternation among the passengers what was about to ensue. Were the officers there to make an arrest? The officers asked everyone to sit still for a few minutes. They slowly made their way down the aisle, looking at the seated passengers, and stopped at the two of us sitting together. They looked at us carefully, as if assessing how dangerous Vivian and I might be. By this time, our faces were nearing the color of our hair.

The lead officer smiled, as if satisfied.

You ladies be good this weekend, you hear? We know all about the two of you.

You do? I asked. Surely, you must have us mistaken for someone else.

Oh, we know who you are, he said. You be careful. Now you're in our town.

The police officers, smiling, turned around and retraced their steps.

The flight attendant hurried over to check on us.

Are you two ladies okay?

Oh, we're fine, I said. I'm a Justice of the Peace. Back home, our police warned us they'd be watching. Either watching us—or watching out for us—I can't be sure which.

On Valentine's Day Vivian and I found a dollar store and bought a pair of cheap wedding bands. We put them on. Then, we walked out to the middle of the bridge that spans the Truckee River. We took the rings off and threw them into the river.

Goodbye! we shouted. Goodbye!

That weekend with Vivian was the beginning of a comeback for both of us. When we arrived at the airport to head home, the tour guide eyed us and asked if we wanted gurneys. I smiled, and declined the offer. We didn't look quite that bad, I thought.

After Vivian and I arrived home, I learned that Cathy

and Shelley had arranged for a family get-together for me at my house. They had invited Sarah and Arlene and their husbands for a barbecue in the back yard. Vivian said she would join us after she finished work.

It was my first meeting with Sarah. I felt nervous and excited at the same time. When I arrived home, I was met at the door by a slight, young woman. Sarah was fair; she had beautiful blue eyes. We immediately embraced. I was surprised by how much alike Sarah and Arlene looked. I could see how others might have thought they were sisters. I shook hands with Sarah and Arlene's husbands. We all sat down eventually, and I talked about my trip.

As the evening progressed, we were having a reasonably good time. The girls and I had been talking about what we had been doing recently. Sarah wasn't working; she was staying at home, taking care of her two daughters. Her husband, Ron, was a manager at an accounting firm. The girls had had several drinks and we were waiting for Vivian to arrive before we sat down to eat.

Sarah started talking about the past and some of the things she had been told about me, and Arlene joined in. They placed the responsibility of their adoption on me. They had been told that I had been an unfit mother. I was surprised and hurt by this turn in the conversation.

At this point, Vivian arrived from work and joined the conversation. She could see how upset I was. I told the girls I would take part of the responsibility for what had happened to them.

I said, If I knew then what I know now, things would have turned out quite differently. Now I was in tears.

Vivien suggested that the best I might be able to do is admit to half the responsibility for what had occurred. Striking a middle ground didn't seem to satisfy the two girls. Arlene said that their dad had been a good father. I said she was mistaken.

From that point on, the conversation got increasingly emotional. The girls became more accusatory. Vivian told the girls they would have to leave if they couldn't show a modicum of respect. Sarah and Arlene told their husbands it was time to go. Without saying anything further, they picked up their things and left.

Vivian came over and sat by me. The party was over. The other girls and Joseph got up and said their goodbyes. Vivian and I watched everyone leave.

That evening was the last time I saw Sarah and Arlene. After they had left, I asked myself what I could have done differently. I wondered if there was something I could have said to bring us together. I felt as though I'd been answering the same accusations all my life. I had even been, for a while, one of the accusers. I couldn't blame myself any more. Nor take the blame head-on.

It was all too much for any of us to deal with, I thought. Too many recriminations. Too many hurt feelings. Too much water under the bridge.

One evening I received a telephone call from Cathy. She said that she and her dad were thinking of hiring Joseph's girl friend, Leslie, to do some accounting in the office. I asked if Leslie had ever worked in accounting. Cathy said no, she hadn't, but that she was willing to train Leslie. I cautioned Cathy to be careful. The books had to be impeccable because government agencies could choose to audit them at any time.

Less than a half hour later, I received a telephone call from my son. He was furious. He screamed that he had found out that I had been talking about his girlfriend behind his back.

Joseph, I don't know what you're talking about, I said.

I told him I had talked with Cathy about training Leslie, and that I had told Cathy it was important that the books were done correctly.

Joseph started to swear.

I'll talk to you later, Joseph, I said, and hung up the phone.

Joseph called right back. He was more furious than before. He directed his swearing at me. It was close and personal.

Quietly I said, Have a good life, Joseph.

I hung up the phone. I wasn't willing to try to make it better. I had had enough. But my exchange with Joseph had left me feeling bereft and alone. I had closed the door on Joseph. I wasn't willing to be the target for his anger. I sat by the phone crying, thinking over what I had done wrong. I didn't phone Joseph back. He didn't phone me.

I have happened to see Joseph a couple of times since our conversation. We have not been able to pick up again. I don't know what it would take to do so. I suppose we would both have to be committed to moving forward. But it seems neither of us has the interest in starting up our relationship again. As connected as we were in the past, both of us seem to have moved on to other commitments of more concern to each of us. It's strange: how close you can be to someone at one point in your life and how distant at another. What changed? I was sure that his father had a lot to do with how Joseph felt towards me. I had heard that Joseph had become very close to his father.

Jerry and Cathy put the business up for sale and were successful in selling it. I witnessed the signature of the documents. Shelley and Roger were living in the Fraser Valley on five acres of land. They had two horses and a couple of dogs and several cats. I invited Shelley and Roger to visit me on many occasions but the invitations were never accepted.

Once, when I was at Shelley's for dinner, she invited Jerry. I am not sure what her thoughts were for bringing us together. Maybe all she hoped for was a family gathering that both her parents could attend. All the time I was there, Jerry kept calling me "dear" and "sweetie". Finally, my temper flared.

My name is Colleen, I said loudly. Please use it. You have lost the right to call me anything else but that.

Needless to say, the evening was lost from that point on. I excused myself and said it was time for me to leave. I had a long drive home ahead of me.

From that date on, Shelley never asked me to her place again or called me. I would call and talk to her but it was always my doing. When she answered, it was always short and to the point. When I closed the conversation, I always said, I love you.

Shelley never responded in kind.

Near Christmas, I got a call from Aunty Gail that Uncle Ray was undergoing triple bypass surgery. I asked whether I should come out to be with them. Aunty Gail assured me that Uncle Ray would be fine. I phoned him at the hospital just before he went into surgery. He sounded less animated than he usually did, but that was not surprising. He seemed in a good mood. I said I would see him soon.

I learned the next day that he had come through the surgery fine. Within two days he was up walking the halls and wanted turkey dinner for Christmas. He was recuperating well. When Christmas came, my aunt made him a turkey dinner. We talked on the telephone almost every day.

It was in February that I received a telephone call from Aunty Gail. She told me that Uncle Ray had been on his way to deliver food to the food bank when he had collapsed. He had died before the ambulance had gotten to him.

I'll come out to Alberta as soon as I can, I said.

No, said Aunty Gail. Just remember him the way he was. You know, that's what he would have wanted.

I agreed. I thought of all the years that I had known my uncle and counted on him. I had counted on his laughter and his supportive words and his strong arms around me. I had loved him dearly and had felt so much love in return.

On the day of his funeral, I felt a presence come to me saying that Uncle Ray was fine and that he loved me. I felt the hot tears in my heart. I heard the phoenix's beautiful song again. The song was saying that Uncle Ray was fine and that there was no reason to worry about him.

It was only a matter of weeks before I got a call from my cousin, Elizabeth, in Alberta. My Aunty Gail had died. My aunt had gone to bed the night before and had passed some time before morning. I had talked to Aunty Gail only a few days before. She had had a slight cold.

I found out when the funeral was and made arrangements to fly to Alberta to join her family. When I arrived in Calgary, Shelley met me at the airport. She and Roger had moved to Alberta several months previously due to Roger's employment. I didn't know what Shelley had been doing but it looked as though she had been working outside. Her nails were black with dirt. I asked her if we were going home to get changed before the funeral. She said no. She said she was going the way she was. I was surprised. I didn't know how Shelley could have stopped digging in the garden and then, without preparing for it, gone to the funeral of a loved one. I was disgusted by the way she was dressed and how dirty she was. I asked myself what she was trying to prove. What did Roger think of her attitude and dress? I decided it was better that I say nothing.

I wore a black skirt, white blouse and black jacket. I thought my aunt would like to see me the way I dressed when I went to court. I felt I understood why Aunty Gail had died. Uncle Ray had never been without her. I felt Uncle Ray must have called her to be with him, and Aunty Gail had responded.

We got to the funeral home and I was asked to sit with Aunty Gail's family. Shelley sat with Roger. He looked very business-like in a suit, shirt and tie. I don't know if Shelley knew how I felt about the way she was dressed. I suspect that she did. She barely spoke to me while I was there.

During the ceremony each member of the family was given a rose to lay beside Aunty Gail. When it was my turn, I went up to the casket. I looked down and I swear my aunt winked at me. I also swear she smiled at me. At the time I thought I was allowing my imagination to go too far. I spoke of the wonderful times we had together and the bond that had been forged between us. I had tears running down my face. And again the song came to me and it was beautiful. I laid the rose over my aunt's hands and again she winked and smiled at me. I looked at my aunt and wished her soul peace and rest. I knew she and Uncle Ray were together.

After the funeral we all went to Uncle Ray and Aunty Gail's house. My cousin, Mike, was there from the island. I hadn't talked to him since our telephone call. We sat together and talked. We discussed what had happened over the years. Of course, I told him that Jerry was no longer in my life.

He said, It was about time.

He asked me how things were going. I said I was managing fairly well. We promised to get together soon.

There were people there from Three Hills also, some whom I sort of knew and others whom I had never met. We had a wonderful time talking. The time came for me to leave for my flight. One of my friends from Three Hills volunteered to drive me to the airport. As I was going to leave, I thanked Shelley for picking me up and spending the day with me.

Shelley never said a word. She turned her back to me and walked away.

From that day to this I have not heard from nor seen Shelley. For many years I sent her a Christmas card and a card remembering her birthday. But, for all I know, she has never received them.

I think of my children often. I think of the very short time I had to love Sarah, Arlene and Colin. I thought often of leaving Jerry but I could never go through with it. Leaving him could have meant losing my family—for a second time. The pain of losing Sarah, Arlene and Colin left me little choice when it came to my "second" family. I would not have given them up for the world.

Yet it has turned out far differently than I had hoped.

I have not spoken to Sarah or Arlene for more than ten years. The last time I saw Colin he was two weeks old. I understand that he has no interest in meeting me. I have already spoken about my relationship with Joseph. I have not seen Shelley in a very long time, nor heard from her. I have been told that Shelley and Roger have separated and are divorcing.

I have had the wonderful opportunity to get to know

Cathy after having lost contact with her for almost ten years. Luckily, we have been reunited and are developing a relationship that is more about being good friends than about being a mother and a daughter. I have a great love for Cathy. She has a heart of gold, and will help anyone she can.

The very first time I saw Cathy after ten years, I cried. She cried, too. We both vowed that whatever might happen we would never be parted again. I love her so much. My heart just expands when I see her. Now I introduce her as my daughter and my friend. We call each other at least once a week. Occasionally, we choose a restaurant and go out for lunch. We do what other daughters and mothers do: we go to each other's home, and we talk about our week, and about what we see coming up. We don't talk very much about the past. I know Cathy feels dearly about her dad. I don't want her to feel she has to choose between her dad and myself. She knows her dad and I hold two very different and opposing versions of the past. It would be unfair to ask her to choose between them. I can understand how she might feel. Having to choose would only bring more heartache.

I can say that someone was looking after me to bring Cathy back in my life. For that I am forever grateful.

Chapter Twenty-One

Sometimes I cry my heart out over the events of my life. I have managed to do what I have done through perseverance. I have been a Justice of the Peace. I have no university degree, just a graduate degree in street smarts.

When I reflect back on my years as Justice of the Peace, I am thankful. Having been a Justice has made me a stronger and more self-assured woman. It has taught me to deal with people—from the highest to the lowest. There is a street lady in Vancouver whom I see every once in a while. I have talked to her on and off for several years. Sometimes when I am walking on the street, she will call out to me: Hello, Judge. I walk across the street to talk to her, just to say hello and tell her to have a good day. She is always dressed nicely. It seems like it is her job to walk around the town and ask for change.

As a Justice I was on duty from Monday to Thursday from four o'clock in the afternoon until eight o'clock in the morning. During that time I might be called in to do bail hearings. With search warrants the police might call and be by my home at any time. I was available from four in the afternoon on Friday until eight in the morning on Monday.

On the weekends I would call each police station and see what lay ahead for the day. I looked after three municipalities and all three of them were very busy.

After I made phone calls, I would sit down with my coffee and think, Oh well, someone has to do this. It might as well be me.

Then I would get up and get ready to go. I would always dress judicially, in black and white, black dress pants or skirt, and white blouse and black jacket.

When I arrived at each police station, I would report to the watch commander's office. Then, it would be to my court room, accompanied by my Crown counsel for the day. My Crown counsel would usually be a corporal in the police force. He would have all the in-custody files with him.

During the day I might handle as many as forty or more cases. With that regimen, time is not a luxury. You make decisions and you weigh the evidence presented to you by Crown and all the facets of the case and make the best determination you can make. In the meantime, you may be interrupted by officers wanting a search warrant, or for that matter, several search warrants.

On any specific day I might handle offences from theft to prostitution to assault. If there was anything I learned in my position, it was to be versatile.

While working as a Justice, I felt lucky when I had the chance to stand down to make a trip to the bathroom or to have a coffee break. As a Justice, you know that if you take too much down time, you will be working much later that day.

Many nights after I finished work all I wanted to do was

soak my bones in a hot bath. The one thing I did learn early on was not to take my work home with me. As soon as I walked out of the court room and bid everyone good night, I pulled a blind down. The day was finished.

If you ponder over the decisions you make in a day, you will never make it as a Justice. You need to be decisive and be strong in the decisions you make. There were many nights when I got home that I was too tired to eat. Then, the telephone would start to ring, with police officers calling for a search warrant.

Hard work? Yes, but I loved it.

During my years as a Justice of the Peace, I dealt with thousands of individual cases. Some are tragic, some funny, and some just make me think: why do people do these things? Often I held people in custody over the weekend so that I could be sure they would appear before a judge on Monday morning. Often they appeared in my courtroom the following weekend. Sometimes it was only a couple of weeks before they were back through the revolving door.

Many times I decided to release a person from custody under certain conditions of release. For example, the alleged accused might be directed to have no contact with the victim of the crime. The accused might be prohibited from being within a certain area of the city or within a certain distance of an establishment.

As a Justice, I heard all kinds of promises. In a couple of months a person might be back in my courtroom for breaching my conditions. Needless to say, I would decide this time to keep him or her in custody.

Other individuals have appeared before me and have regretted the mistakes they have made. There have been times when I have given them the benefit of the doubt and released them from custody. Following their court date, I have never seen them again.

One day while I was downtown, I heard the words "Your Worship". I turned around. A man whom I did not recognize came up to me.

You had me in your court a couple of years ago, he said. I want to thank you.

For what? I asked.

I got the help I needed, he said. I have a responsible job. I'm married. I've got kids and I'm doing pretty well.

He shook my hand and asked if he could give me a hug.

Sure, I said.

In a lot of ways, Your Worship, I owe you my life, he said.

There are not many children that are brought to court. The occasions when they do appear are of special note.

One morning I was having coffee before we started court. My Crown counsel came into the room. He had another man with him. It was surprising that Crown would be bringing someone forward before court had started for the day.

Your Worship, he said, I'm sorry to disturb you.

What is it? I asked.

Your Worship, he said, this man would like your help with his son.

I looked at the man. He seemed sincerely distressed.

How old is the boy? I asked.

He's eight, Crown answered.

Why are you here? I asked the father.

My son has been stealing money, he said. Whatever I do hasn't stopped him. Please, I am here to ask for your help before I lose him totally.

What is it you want me to do with your son? There are no

charges against him.

If you would be tough on him, maybe . . .

You mean like "tough love"?

Yes. If you would, please help us before it's too late.

Do I have your permission to speak so with your son?

Yes, you do.

All right, I'll see what I can do. Crown, is there a cell available in the Young Offenders wing?

Yes, there is.

Fine, I said, escort the father out until we're finished. Then bring in the boy.

In a few minutes, Crown accompanied a small boy into the room. He was a tiny boy, one who looked like he couldn't steal anything.

The boy went to sit down.

You will stand, I said, and you will take your hands out of your pockets.

He did as he was told.

Crown, I asked, Why is this boy here?

Theft, Your Worship, Crown replied.

What is your name? I asked.

The boy told me.

Where do you live?

The boy gave his address.

Do you go to school?

Yes.

Do you go to school every day?

Yes.

Fine, I said. Crown, let's go downstairs.

I whispered to Crown my instructions.

I had Crown lead us. We descended the stairs in single file: Crown, the boy, followed by myself.

Crown opened a cell door. The boy and I entered.

As I had instructed, Crown slammed the cell door shut. The cell door made such a loud noise it even scared me.

I motioned the boy to the concrete bed. We sat down together.

I'm taking my hat off. While we are here, I am not a Justice. I am here to listen to you and to help you if I can. Now, please tell me what the problem is.

The boy started to cry. He said there were bigger boys at school. If he didn't bring these boys money or candy every day, they would beat him up.

He was crying hard. I asked him if I could put my arms around him.

Yes, he said.

He began to sob.

I asked him where his mom was.

Gone, he said. I don't know where.

Have you told your dad what's been going on? I asked.

I'm too scared to tell him, he said.

Well then, I said, I will have to do it. Come on, it's time now to go upstairs and talk to your dad.

I called Crown. He let us out of the cell and we walked back up the stairs. I held the boy's hand in mine. Before going into court, I stopped and wiped the tears from his face.

I called the boy's father into the court room. I had the boy by my side.

Did you know your son was being bullied, beaten up if he didn't bring money to school?

The father stood there with his mouth open. He said he had no idea of what had been happening but he promised that he would take care of it the very next day.

I said to the father, I will take you on your word that you will look after this problem. This little boy has enough problems in his young life. He doesn't need any more.

I asked Crown to give the boy his business card. I wrote my name down on the back of it.

If you ever need me, I said to the boy, just call this number. Mention my name. The police will come and pick you up. I will be there as soon as I can.

That was fifteen years ago. I never heard from the boy or his father again.

I expect that, like myself, they have not forgotten their day in court.

One weekend day, while I was Justice in court, Crown brought a fourteen-year-old girl before me. She looked about ten years old. She was wearing a Winnie the Pooh t-shirt with ruffles. She was so short that she didn't even come up to the top of the bench. I really wondered if there could be any reason for bringing such a sweet looking girl into court. When I asked for the charge against the girl, Crown replied that she was charged with operating a marijuana grow-op.

Where are her parents? I asked.

There are no parents here, Crown replied.

Is there anyone to be with her during this hearing? I asked.

No, said Crown.

Why not? I asked.

Could we stand down, Your Worship? asked the Crown.

Fine, I said. Please put the girl in a safe place until we can resume.

When Crown returned, he said, Your Worship, there are warrants for her arrest from here to Alberta. When she was arrested, she had in her possession a .357 magnum—with a silencer on it. And I'm told she knew how to use it.

With that information before me, I changed my mind. I remanded the young girl into custody.

One day the police brought in a woman who had been drinking. I anticipated a charge against her of driving under the influence. But the woman had not been driving. The police officers had happened on her, asleep in her car with the keys in the ignition. The officers simply had brought her in for her own good.

As she had not been charged, the officers placed her in a cell to sleep off the alcohol. The woman had a wicker basket with her and she took it with her into the cell. The officers thought they had better see what was in the basket. When they opened it, out jumped a beautiful long-haired orange cat.

The cat proceeded to wander the cell area and made friends with everyone. It was only a matter of time until the cat ended up in the court room. The cat jumped on my bench and tiptoed among my documents and plunked down, as cats always do, right in the middle of the documents I was examining. He started to purrrrrrrrrr. I like you I like you. And, as cats do, when they want to be close to someone, the cat nudged me and purred.

I like you also, I addressed the cat, but would you mind not sitting on my documents as I have to read them.

The cat looked at me with love but refused to move.

What am I going to do with you? I asked.

When the next case was brought forward, the cat's fur stood up on end. He started to hiss. I looked at the fellow before me and decided to have the cat taken from the court. I decided to proceed with the door closed. I had the feeling that if the alleged accused had made one wrong move he would have ended up with claws in his chest. After I'd had a chance to look over the documents regarding the case, I thought the cat's reactions were justified. I thought, Even a cat can tell who his friends are.

Sometimes, between seeing cases, I thought to myself, I have been to hell and back but here I am in a position of trust and authority. I have had no one to help me make the decisions I have made. Here I am a Justice. I could be as easily standing on the other side of my bench, one of the people I see every weekend. I truly believe that someone has been with me to help in the decisions I have made. I am not educated. I left school, and married very young. Yet ever since I can remember, I have wanted to be a criminal lawyer. I could have been a prostitute or a drug addict quite easily, but here I am sitting in a court room, trying to do my best to help people.

Every time I have been knocked off my feet I have risen out of the ashes, just like the Phoenix. That is what I will continue to do until Spirit takes me home.

On a Sunday morning at 5:15, I woke out of a sound sleep and got out of bed. I walked barefoot into the living room. I didn't turn any lights on. As I walked to the front window, I was taken by what I saw. The view was stunning, like so many diamonds shimmering in the night. The city of Vancouver was full of thousands of twinkling lights, diamonds in the early morning darkness.

As I stood looking out, a feeling of serenity and calm overtook me. I thought of how lucky I am to be living free.

Then looking to the east and through the darkness of the night, I saw the most beautiful streak of blue just peeking through the night sky. As I stood watching the sky start to open, I saw the blue sky start to take its place. And a feeling of extreme peace came over me, a feeling that Spirit was watching, almost holding my heart. I stood watching the sky start to lighten for another day, one of hope and promise.

Afterword

I wish to thank those who have supported me in the writing of my story and who have encouraged me to tell it.

There have been others who have heard my story and have had trouble believing it. They say: surely, even years ago, social workers couldn't just walk into your home and take your children. Surely, social workers, before apprehending one's children, carried out a careful investigation and followed due process of law. Surely, even as a young mother, I must have had the opportunity to hear the accusations against me and been encouraged to bring forward evidence to refute them.

These same questions have plagued me. Many times I've imagined how differently I would have handled these events had I known at the time what I know now. And I have had terrible moments when I have questioned my own naivete and lack of confidence, and how these contributed to the events I've related.

Looking back, I'm surprised, too—by how quickly the social workers acted in apprehending my children and the degree to which my protests were ignored. If the information I was given is correct, the social workers involved did carry out a "careful investigation". They did corroborate the accusations made against me with hard evidence. They did follow a deliberative process, of a kind. How? On the first-hand evidence given to them by my husband.

In light of this, the course of events which occurred makes complete sense. The social workers didn't act with undue haste, after all. They met and talked with my husband on a number of occasions. They verified the accusations made against me. And they carried out a plan how my children would be "cared for". If this were so, my husband's indifference and unconcern at the time are completely understandable. While I was unprepared for the events that were about to occur, he was aware of the order in which they would transpire.

Missing in all of this was the frank and open discussion that should have occurred—with me. I have no way of confirming many details of my story. I have requested government documents in regard to my children's apprehension and have been told by officials that these documents no longer exist.

I have tried to understand my life. That is the most anyone of us can do. I have tried to understand my mother's lack of feeling towards me and her hate of my father. I have tried to understand my mother's feelings of entrapment and of missed opportunity, and her deep-seated resentment. My mother felt she had been trapped by the choices she had made: having married a man below her station, a drunk and a layabout, having borne and raised a child when she wanted none, and having divorced in an era when divorce was more the exception than the rule.

I have presented my story as best I can, and recognize that it is sadly incomplete. I wish I knew more of its details. I believe knowing these details would help me understand some of the events that have occurred and allow me to put them to rest. But, as is often the case with loss, some things remain unresolved. Even, after all I have told, a part of my story must remain a mystery—even to me.

Acknowledgments

This book was written with the encouragement and support of many wonderful friends:

My editor and friend, Phil Rivest, who encouraged me to write my story and not to stop until it was complete. Without his help this book would not have been written.

John L. Daly, the first person to see my beginning manuscript, and who continued to encourage me through its writing. Thank you John for never doubting me.

Philippe Brunel, whose technical assistance in formatting the manuscript and preparing the book cover, was outstanding, and generously given.

Liam Rivest, my young gentleman friend, for being who he is.

Lorraine Murphy, my friend and adviser.

Calvin Patterson for encouraging me throughout my journey of discovery.

Al and Gail Jones, who never doubted my abilities.

About the Author

Colleen O'Connor was a Criminal Court Justice of the Peace for the Province of British Columbia for eighteen years. She is a business consultant and resides in Vancouver. She is currently writing her second book.

To contact Colleen O'Connor

write to: Cat's Eye Enterprises Ltd.,
2-2314 West Broadway Street
Vancouver, BC V6K2E5

or e-mail: cryofthephoenix@shaw.ca